the **2000s**

RECORDED VERSIONS
GUITAR

**AUTHENTIC TRANSCRIPTIONS
WITH NOTES & TABLATURE**

W9-CNK-166

ISBN 0-634-09176-X

**HAL•LEONARD®
CORPORATION**

7777 W. BLUEMOUND RD. P.O. BOX 13819 MILWAUKEE, WI 53213

Visit Hal Leonard Online at
www.halleonard.com

the **2000s**

CONTENTS

Aerials

Words and Music by Daron Malakian and Serj Tankian

Gtrs. 1, 2 & 3: Drop D tuning, down 1 step:
(low to high) C-G-C-F-A-D

Gtr. 4: DADGAD tuning, down 1 step:
(low to high) C-G-C-F-G-C

Intro
Free time

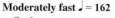

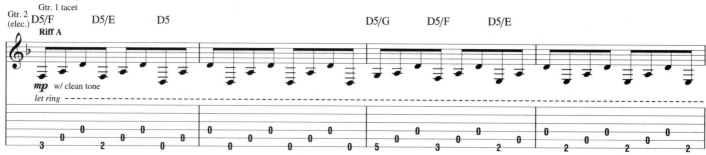

* Strings arr. for gtr. (1st notes begin over end of previous track.)
** Chord symbols reflect implied harmony.

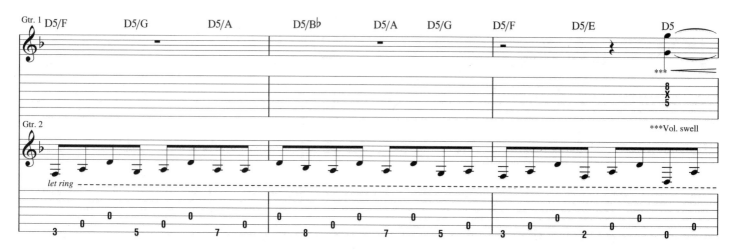

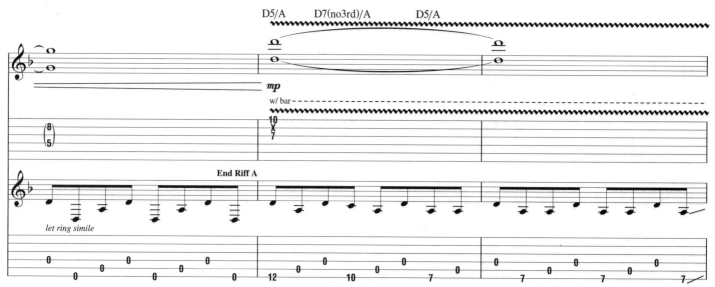

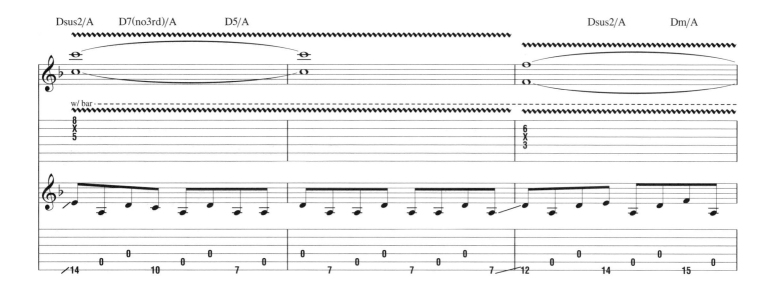

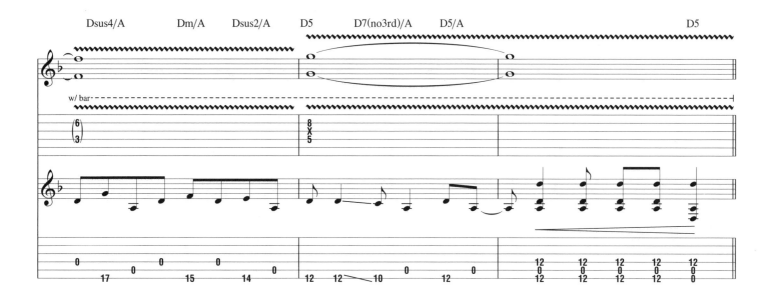

𝄋 Verse

Half-time feel

Gtrs. 1 & 2 tacet
2nd time, Gtr. 4 tacet

1., 2. Life is a wa - ter - fall, — { we're one in the riv - er and one _____ a - gain af - ter the fall. _____

we drink from the riv - er, then we turn a - round and put up our walls. _____ }

* Gtr. 3
(elec.) **Rhy. Fig. 1**

f

w/ dist.

* Doubled throughout

Swim - ming through the void we hear ____ the word, ____ we lose our - selves ___ but we

find it all. ____ 'Cause

we are the ones that wan - na play, ____ al - ways wan - na go but you

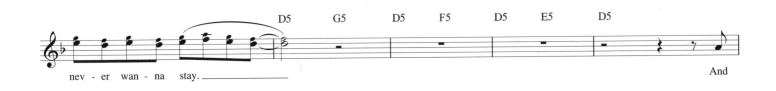

nev - er wan - na stay. ____ And

To Coda ⊕

we are the ones that wan - na choose, ____ al - ways wan - na play but you nev - er wan - na lose. ____

Interlude

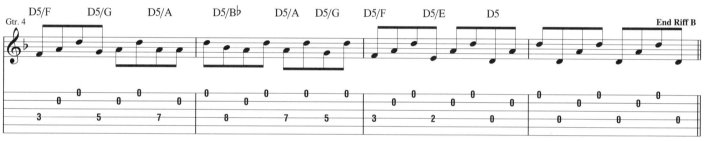

Chorus

Aer - i - als ____ in the ____ sky. ____

When you ____ lose ____ small ____ mind, you free ____ your ____ life. ____

⊕ Coda

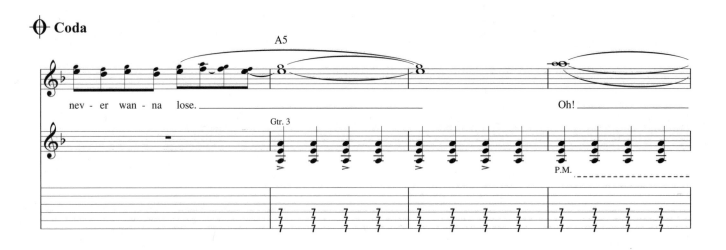

nev - er wan - na lose._____ Oh!_____

Interlude

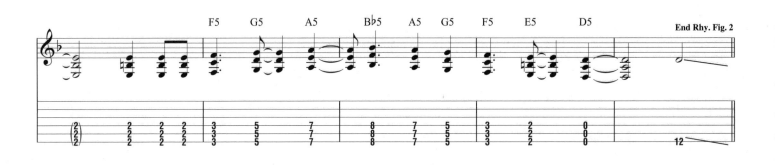

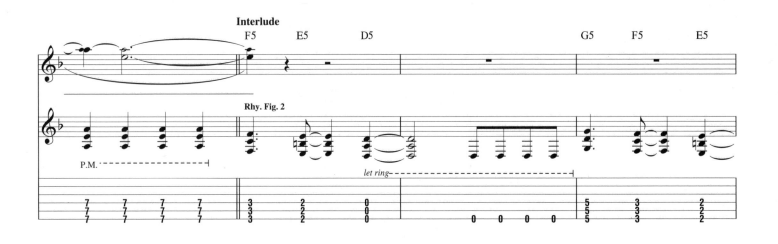

Chorus

Gtr. 3: w/ Rhy. Fig. 2 (2 times)

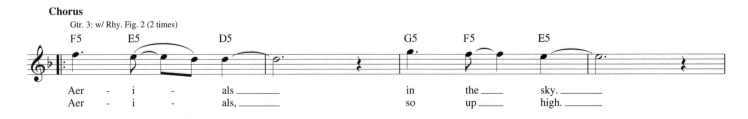

Aer - i - als_____ in the ____ sky._____
Aer - i - als,_____ so up ____ high._____

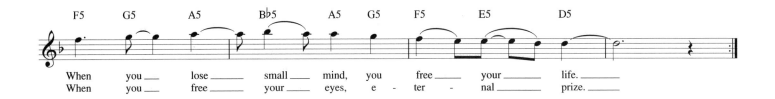

When you — lose — small — mind, you — free — your — life.
When you — free — your — eyes, e - ter - nal — prize.

Chorus

Gtrs. 2 & 4: w/ Riffs A & B (2 times)

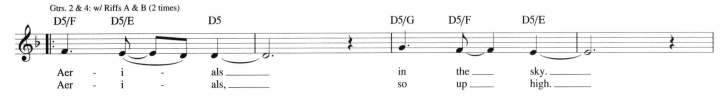

Aer - i - als — in the — sky. —
Aer - i - als, — so up — high. —

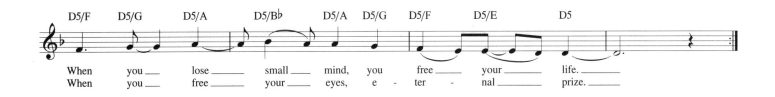

When you — lose — small — mind, you free — your — life. —
When you — free — your — eyes, e - ter - nal — prize. —

Outro

Gtrs. 2 & 4: w/ Riffs A & B (1 3/4 times)

Ah, — ah. — Ah. —

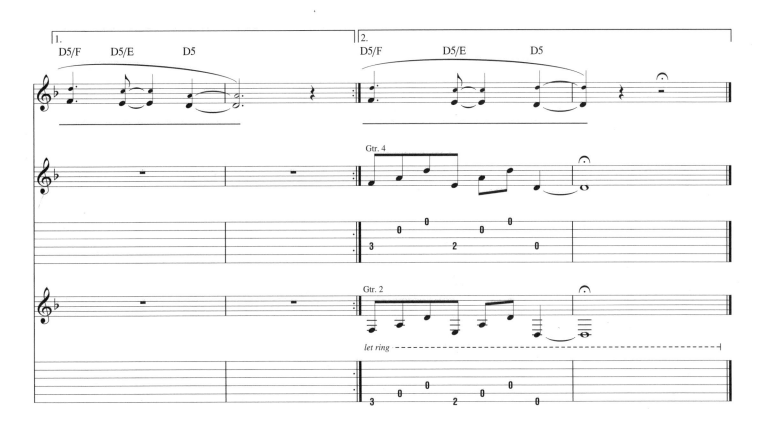

Alive

Words and Music by Sonny, Marcos, Traa and Wuv

Drop D tuning, down 1 step:
(low to high) C-G-C-F-A-D

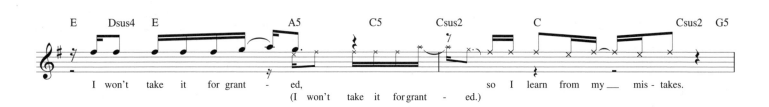

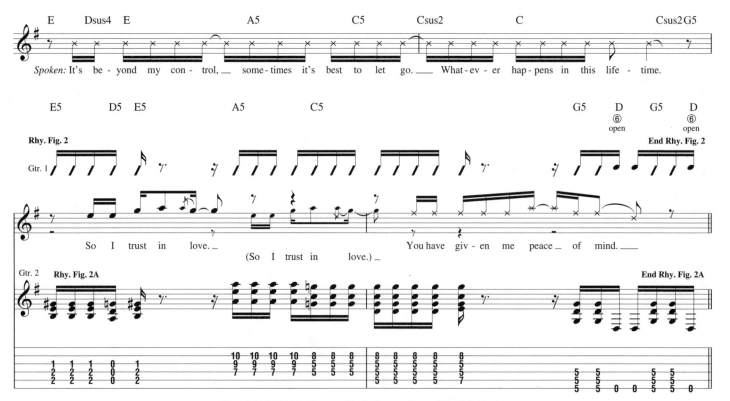

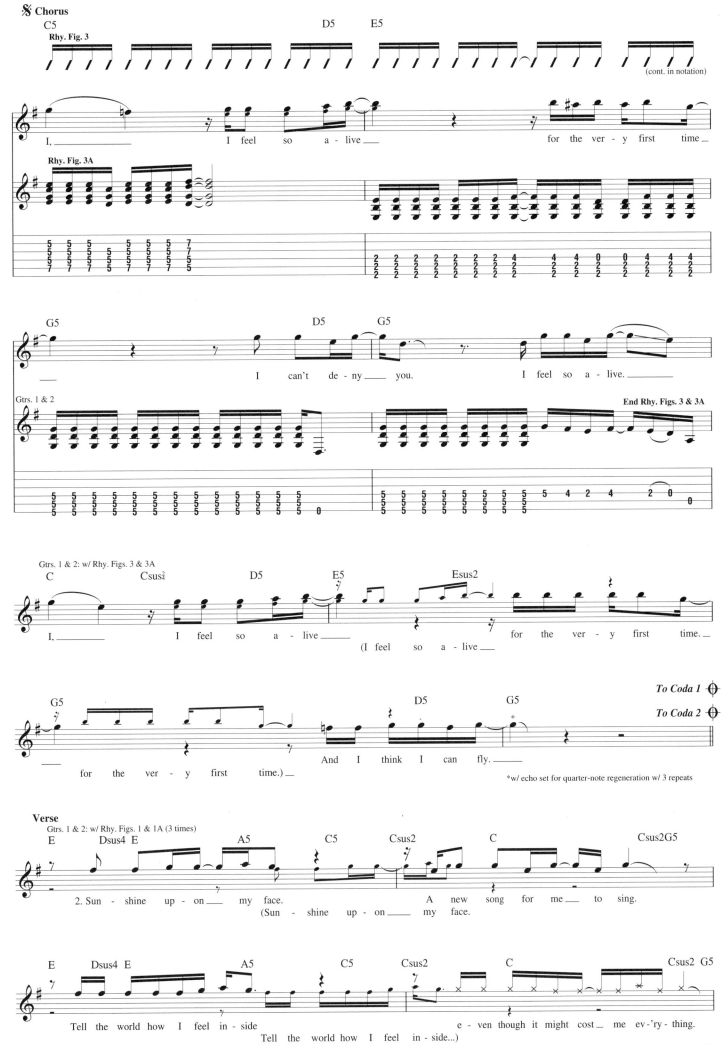

All My Life

Words and Music by Foo Fighters

G5

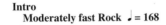

Intro
Moderately fast Rock ♩ = 168

Gtr. 1 (dist.)   N.C.(G5)

Rhy. Fig. 1   **End Rhy. Fig. 1**

P.M. -|

Gtr. 1: w/ Rhy. Fig. 1 (3 ¾ times)

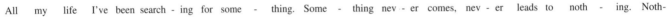

All my life I've been search - ing for some - thing. Some - thing nev - er comes, nev - er leads to noth - ing. Noth-

- ing sat - is - fies but I'm get - ting close, ___ clos - er to the prize ___ at the end of the rope. ___

All night long ___ I dream ___ of the day. ___ When ___ it comes a - round, and it's tak - en a - way. ___ Leaves ___

___ me with the feel - ing that I feel the most, ___ feel ___ it come to life when I

Interlude
Gm   Am

see your ghost. ___

Gtr. 1

Gtrs. 1 & 2
(dist.)

P.M. - - - - - - - - - - - - - - -| Harm.

f

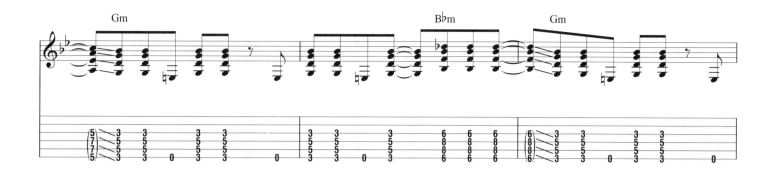

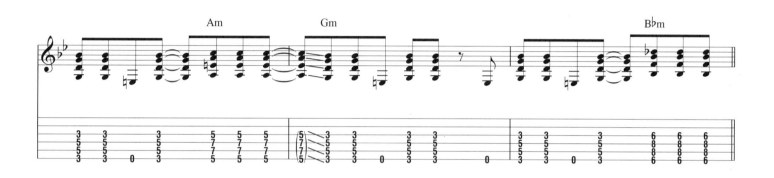

Verse

1. Calm down, don't you re - sist. You've such a del - i - cate wrist. __
2. Will I find __ a be - liev - er, __ an - oth - er one who be - lieves, __

Rhy. Fig. 2

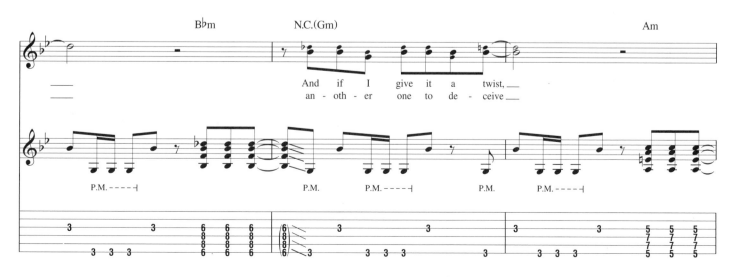

And if I give it a twist, __
an - oth - er one to de - ceive

some-thing to hold when I lose my grip. ___
o - ver and o - ver down on my knees? ___

Will I find ___ some - thing in

there
er

to give me just what I need? ___
and if you o - pen up wide, ___

An - oth - er rea - son to bleed, ___
and if you let me in - side ___

one by one hid - den
on and on I got

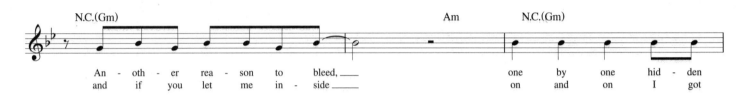

up my sleeve. ___
noth - ing to hide. ___

One by one hid - den up my sleeve. ___
On and on I got noth - ing to hide. ___

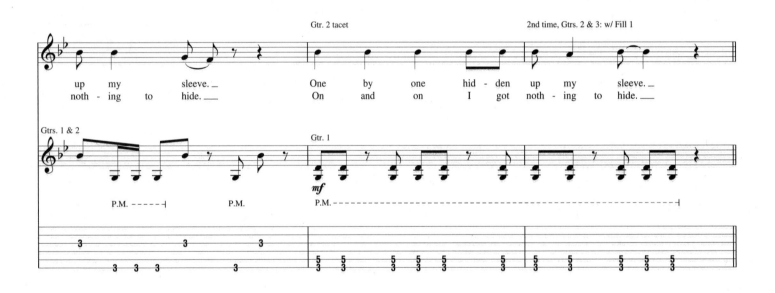

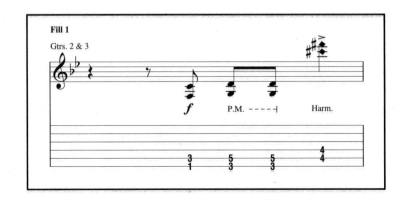

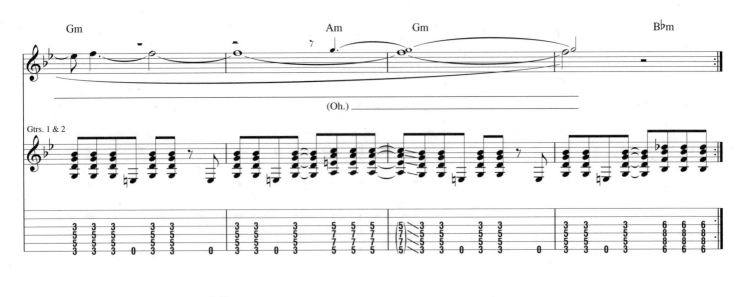

(Oh.)

Gtrs. 1 & 2

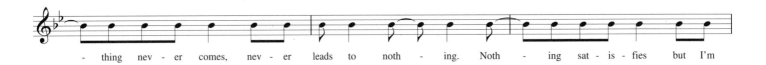

Bridge

Gtr. 1: w/ Rhy. Fig. 1 (2 times)
Gtr. 2 tacet
N.C.(G5)

Gtr. 1: w/ Rhy. Fig. 1 (1 ¾ times)
Gtrs. 2 & 3: w/ Fill 2 (8 times)
N.C.(G5)

All my life I've been search - ing for some - thing. Some -

- thing nev - er comes, nev - er leads to noth - ing. Noth - ing sat - is - fies but I'm

Gtr. 1: w/ Rhy. Fill 1

get - ting close, ___ clos - er to the prize ___ at the end of the rope. ___

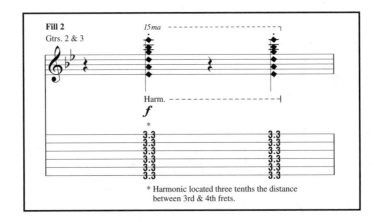

Fill 2
Gtrs. 2 & 3

15ma

Harm.

f

* Harmonic located three tenths the distance
between 3rd & 4th frets.

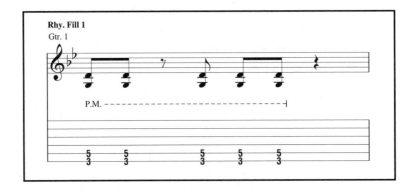

Rhy. Fill 1
Gtr. 1

P.M.

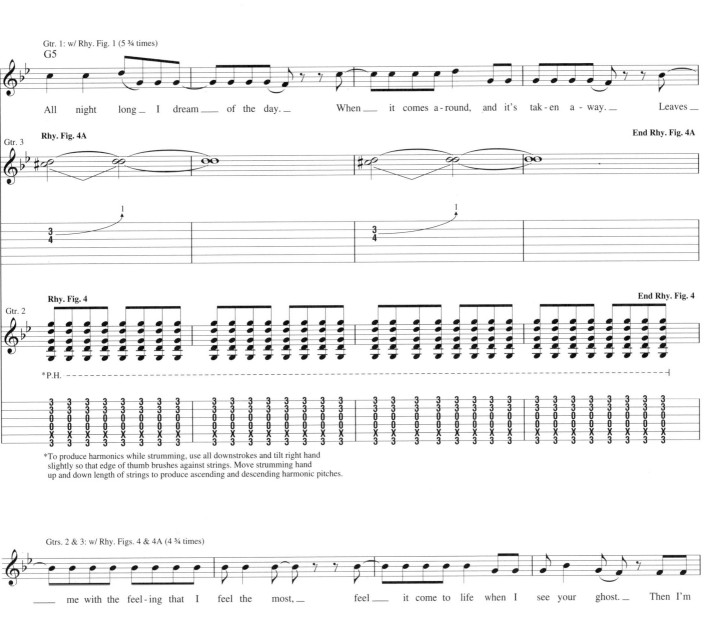

Gtr. 1: w/ Rhy. Fig. 1 (5 ¾ times)

G5

All night long I dream of the day. When it comes a-round, and it's tak-en a-way. Leaves

Rhy. Fig. 4A
Gtr. 3
End Rhy. Fig. 4A

Rhy. Fig. 4
Gtr. 2
End Rhy. Fig. 4

*P.H.

*To produce harmonics while strumming, use all downstrokes and tilt right hand
slightly so that edge of thumb brushes against strings. Move strumming hand
up and down length of strings to produce ascending and descending harmonic pitches.

Gtrs. 2 & 3: w/ Rhy. Figs. 4 & 4A (4 ¾ times)

me with the feel-ing that I feel the most, feel it come to life when I see your ghost. Then I'm

done, done, on to the next one. Done, done and I'm

on to the next one. Done, done and I'm on to the next one. Done,

done and I'm on to the next one. Done, done and I'm

on to the next one. Done, done and I'm on to the next one. Done,

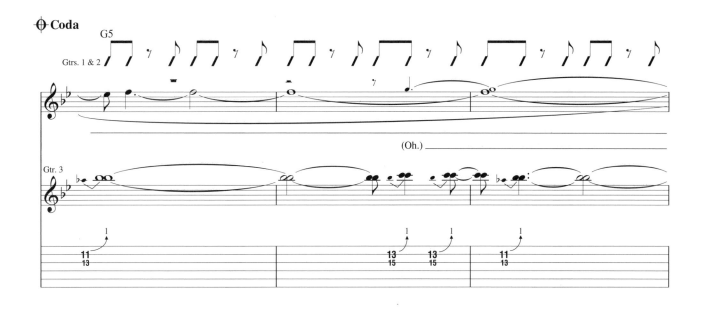

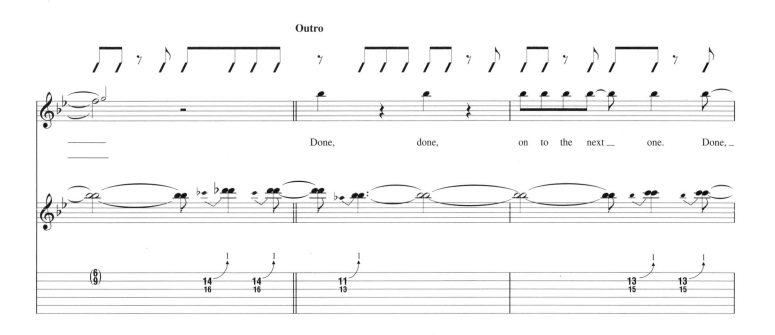

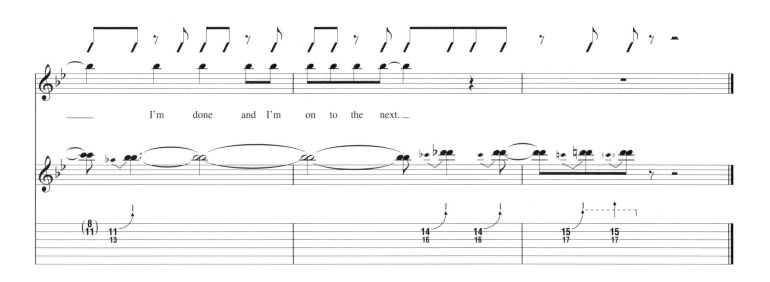

All the Small Things

Words and Music by Tom De Longe and Mark Hoppus

Chorus

Interlude

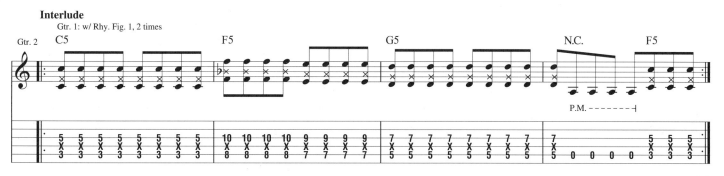

Verse

Gtr. 1: w/ Rhy. Fig. 2
Gtr. 2 tacet

2. Late night, come home. Work sucks, I know.

D.S. al Coda

Gtr. 1: w/ Rhy. Fig. 3

She left me ros - es by the stairs. Sur - pris - es let me know she cares.

Coda

Interlude

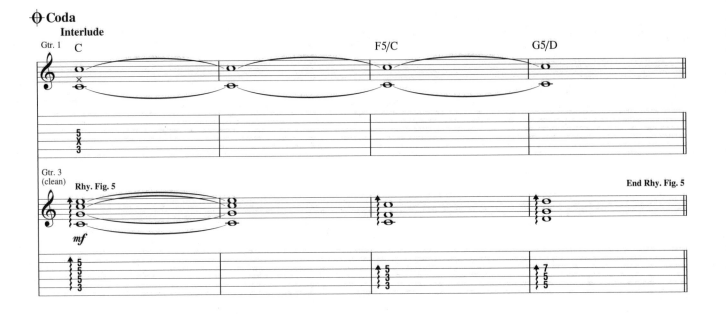

Gtr. 3: w/ Rhy. Fig. 5, 3 times

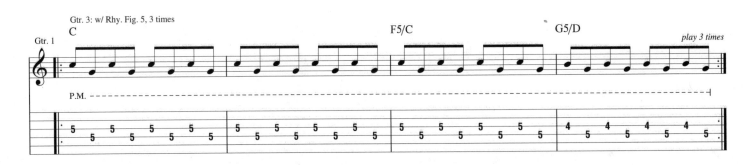

Outro

Gtr. 1: w/ Rhy. Fig. 4, 2 times
Gtr. 2: w/ Riff A, 3 ½ times

Say it ain't so. I will not ___ go. Turn the lights ___ off. Car - ry me ___

home. Keep your head still. I'll be your ___ thrill. The night will go ___ on, my lit - tle wind -

Are You Gonna Be My Girl

Words and Music by Nic Cester and Cameron Muncey

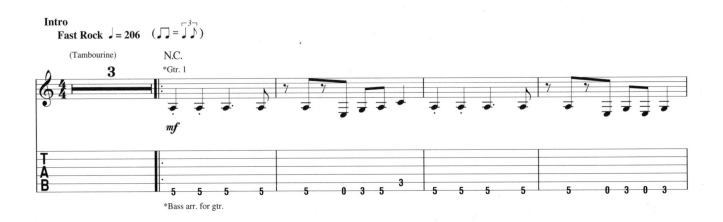

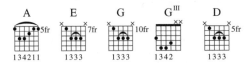

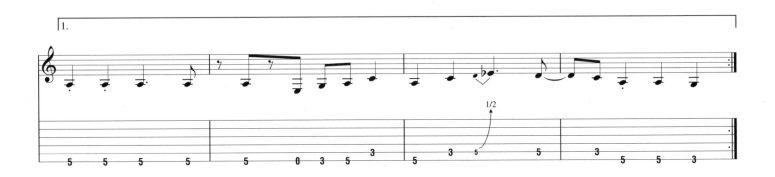

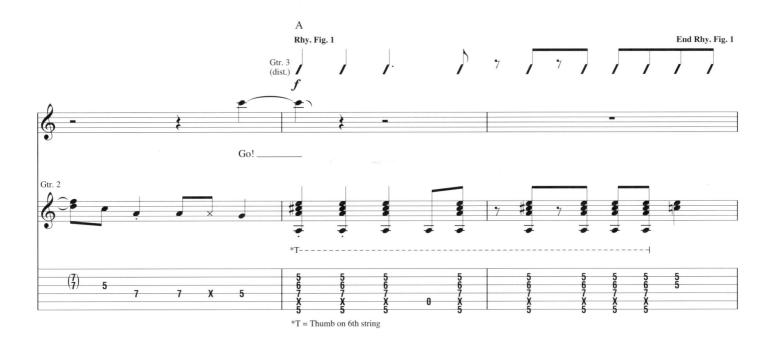

*T = Thumb on 6th string

Gtr. 3: w/ Rhy. Fig. 1 (2 times)

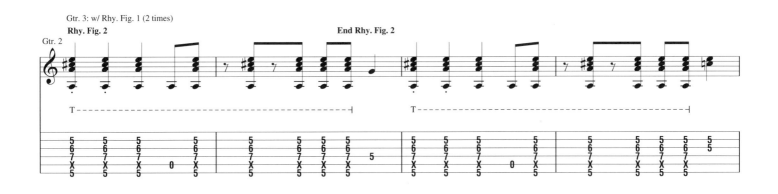

Gtrs. 2 & 3 tacet

hand and come with me be - cause you look so fine and I real - ly want to make you mine.

Gtr. 3: w/ Rhy. Fig. 1

I say you look so fine and I real - ly want to make you mine.

Gtr. 3: w/ Rhy. Fig. 1

Well, four, five, six, come on __

Gtrs. 2 & 3 tacet

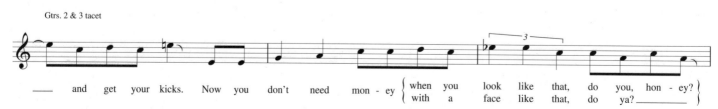

__ and get your kicks. Now you don't need mon - ey { when you look like that, do you, hon - ey? }
{ with a face like that, do ya? __ }

Gtr. 3: w/ Rhy. Fig. 1

Gtr. 3: w/ Riff A

Pre-Chorus

Gtrs. 2 & 3: w/ Rhy. Fig. 4 (2 times)

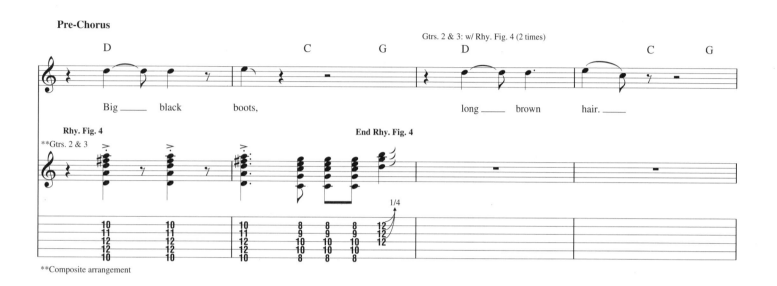

Big _____ black boots, long _____ brown hair. _____

**Composite arrangement

She's _____ so sweet with _____ her get _____ back stare.

Chorus

Well, I could see _____ you home with me, _____

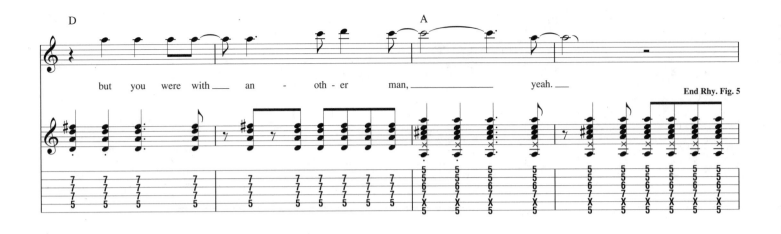

but you were with___ an - oth - er man,_____ yeah.___

End Rhy. Fig. 5

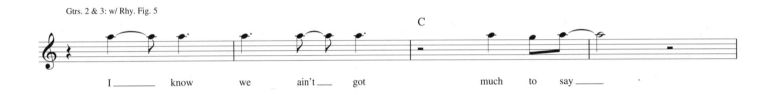

Gtrs. 2 & 3: w/ Rhy. Fig. 5

I _____ know we ain't ___ got much to say _____

be - fore I let _____ you get a - way,_____ yeah. ___

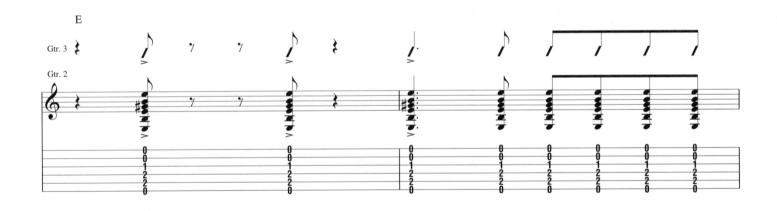

Gtr. 3

Gtr. 2

1.

I said, "Are you gon - na be my girl?" ___

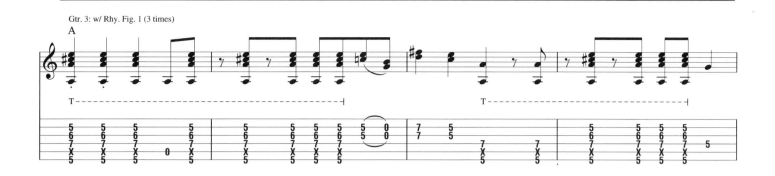

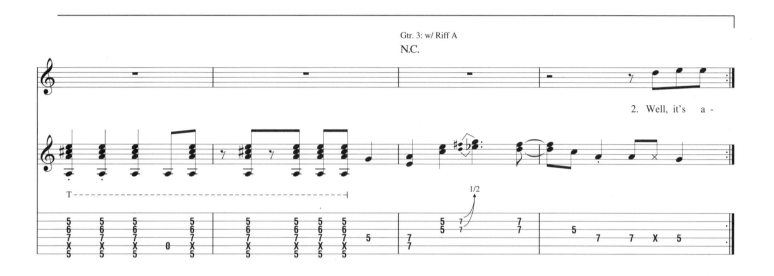

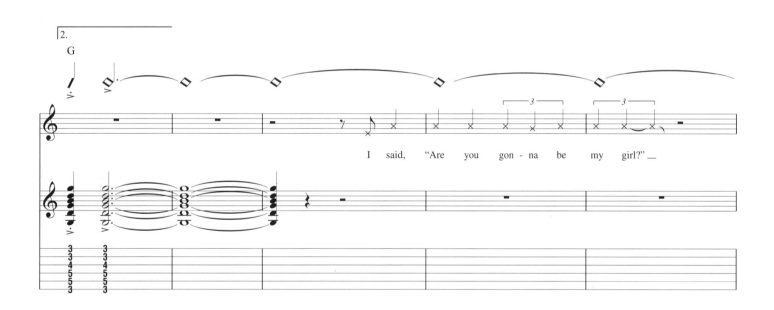

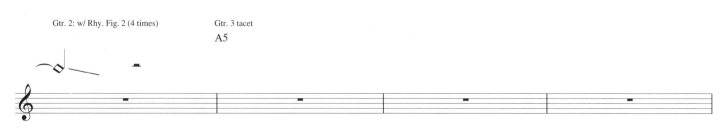

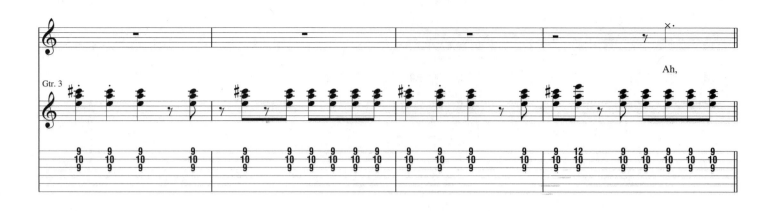

Guitar Solo

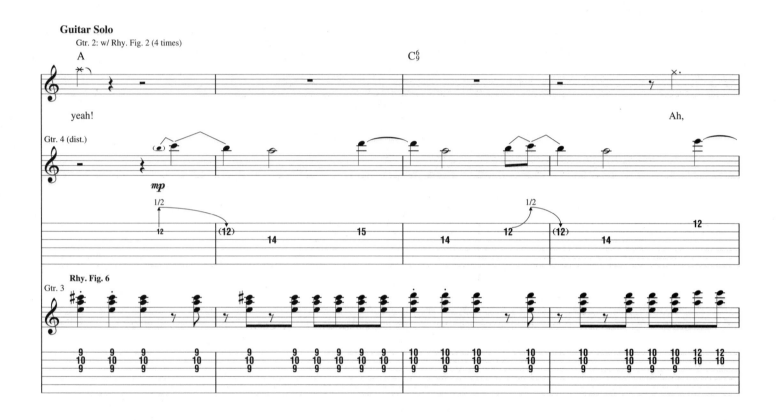

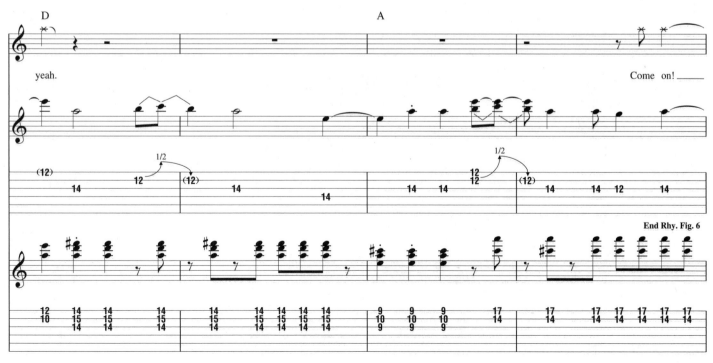

Gtr. 3: w/ Rhy. Fig. 5 (1st 6 meas.)

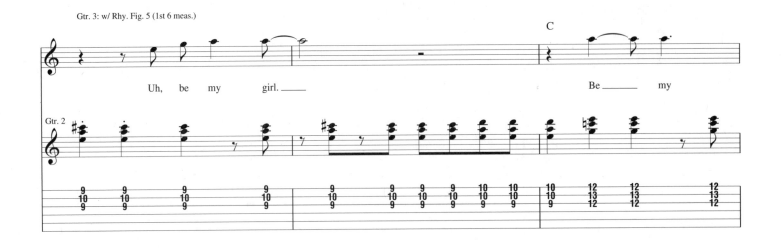

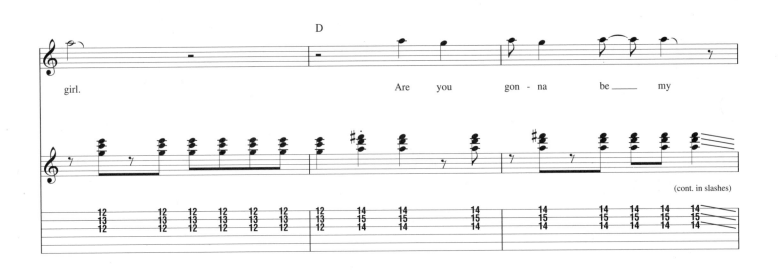

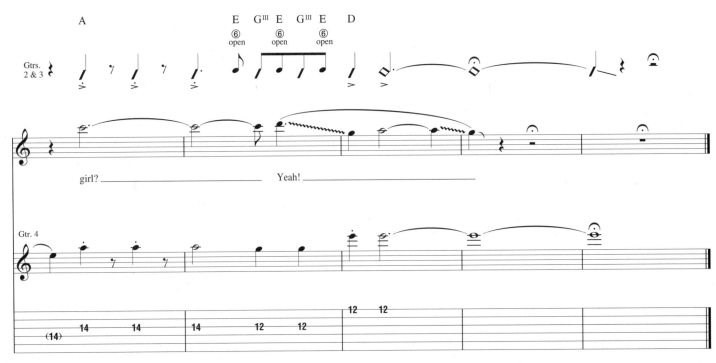

Awake

Words and Music by Sully Erna

Drop D tuning, tune down 1 step:
(low to high) C-G-C-F-A-D

Intro
Moderate Rock ♩ = 110

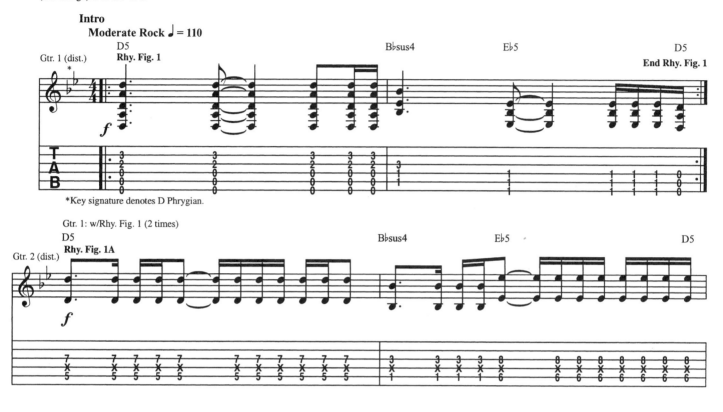

*Key signature denotes D Phrygian.

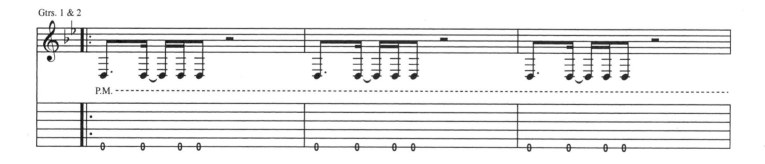

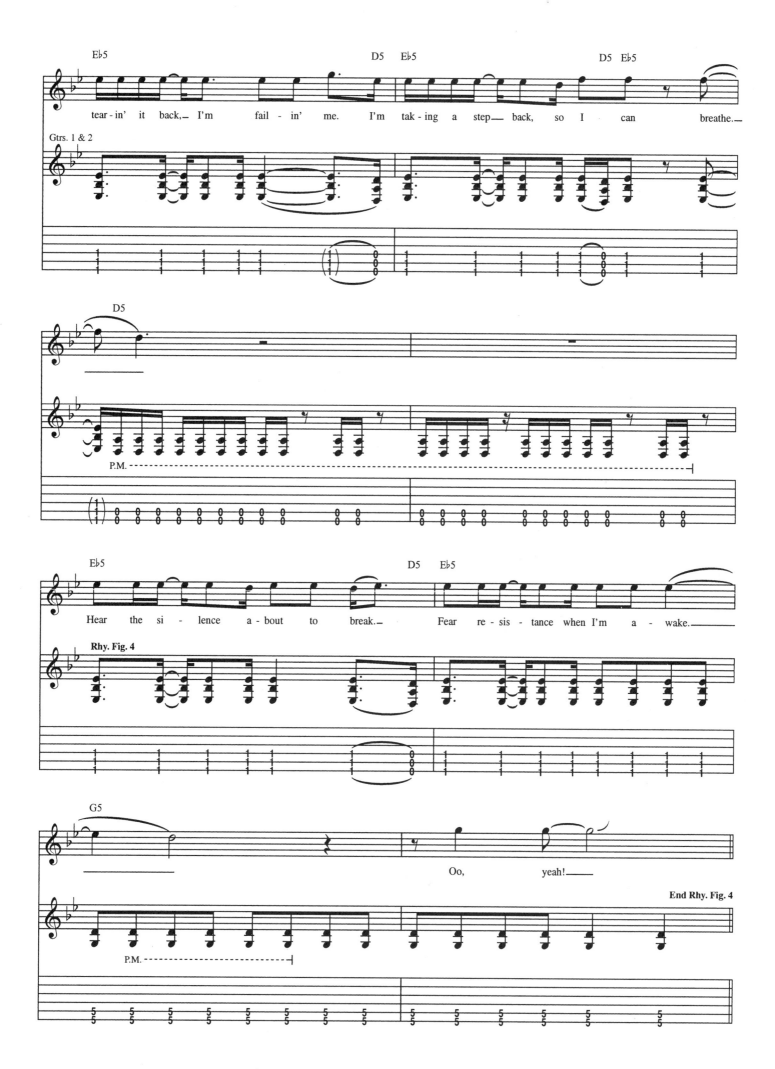

Californication

Words and Music by Anthony Kiedis, Flea, John Frusciante and Chad Smith

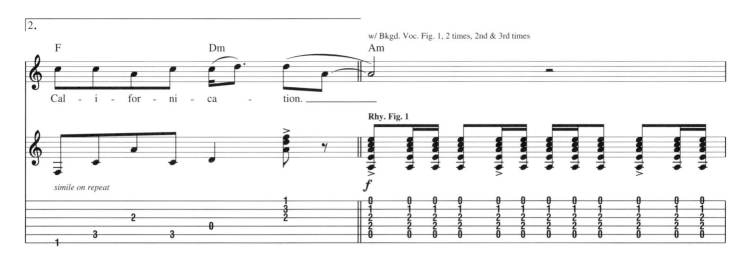

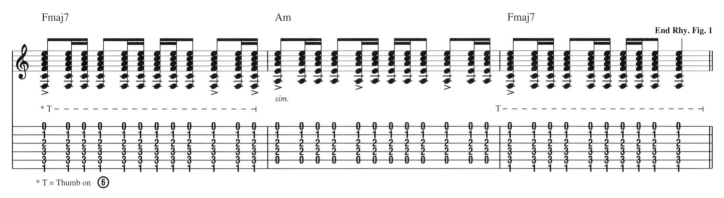

* T = Thumb on ⑥

Pre-Chorus

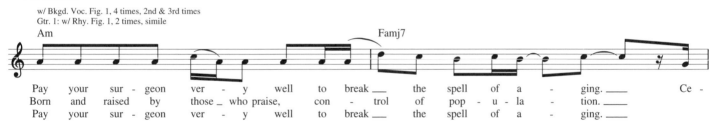

Pay your sur - geon ver - y well to break the spell of a - ging. Ce -
Born and raised by those who praise, con - trol of pop - u - la - tion.
Pay your sur - geon ver - y well to break the spell of a - ging.

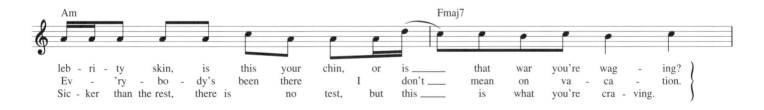

leb - ri - ty skin, is this your chin, or is that war you're wag - ing?
Ev - 'ry - bo - dy's been there I don't mean on va - ca - tion.
Sic - ker than the rest, there is no test, but this is what you're cra - ving.

First born un - i - corn, hard - core soft porn.

Bkgd. Voc. Fig. 1

(Ooh.)

* Slight vibrato throughout.

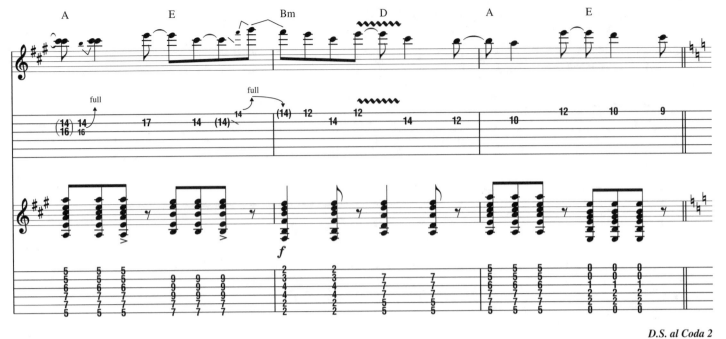

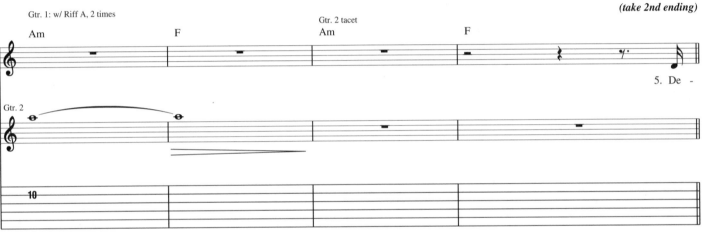

D.S. al Coda 2
(take 2nd ending)

Additional Lyrics

4. Space may be the final frontier,
   But it's made in a Hollywood basement;
   Cobain can you hear the spheres
   Singing songs off station to station.
   And Alderon's not far away;
   It's Californication.

5. Destruction leads to a very rough road
   But it also breeds creation;
   And earthquakes are to a girl's guitar,
   They're just another good vibration
   And tidal waves couldn't save the world
   From Californication.

Click Click Boom

Words and Music by Josey Scott, Chris Dabaldo, Wayne Swinney, Dave Novotny, Paul Crosby and Bob Marlette

_____ it in ___ my ___ mind, _____ I can see _____ it in ___ their ___ eyes.
-ed up ___ my ___ mind? ___ Why's my moth - er al - ways right? _
ooh.

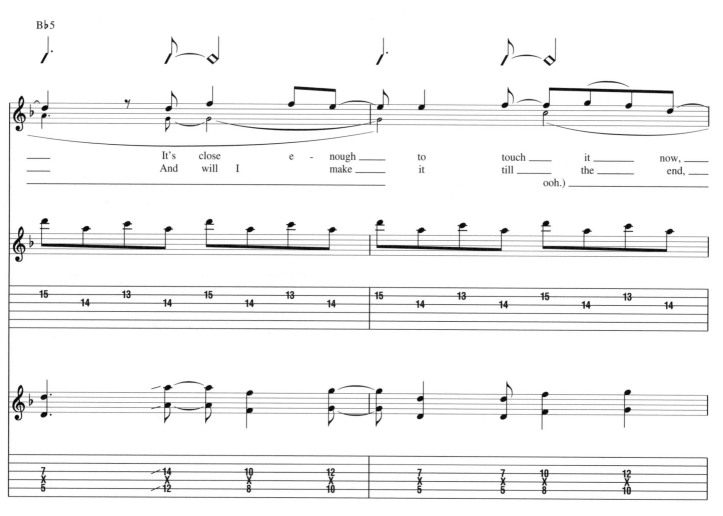

_____ It's close e - nough _____ to touch ____ it _____ now, _____
_____ And will I make _____ it till _____ the _____ end, __
ooh.) _____

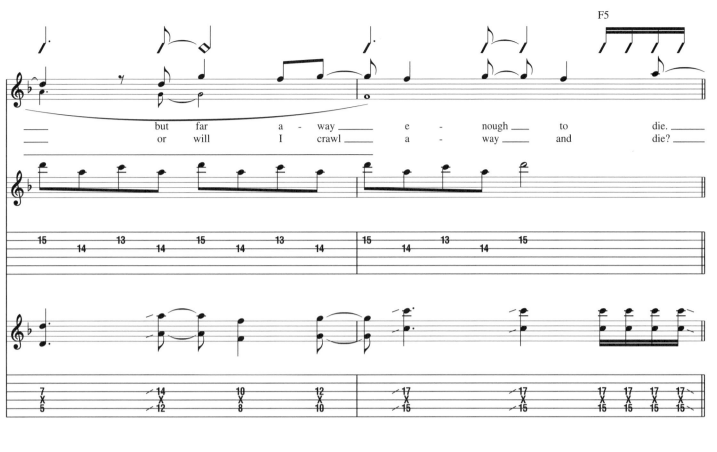

but far a - way ___ e - nough ___ to die. ___
or will I crawl ___ a - way ___ and die? ___

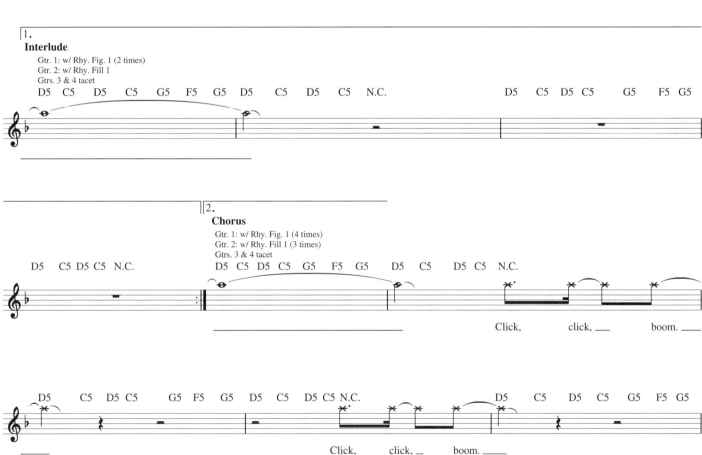

Click, click, ___ boom. ___

Click, click, ___ boom. ___

Click, click, ___ boom. ___

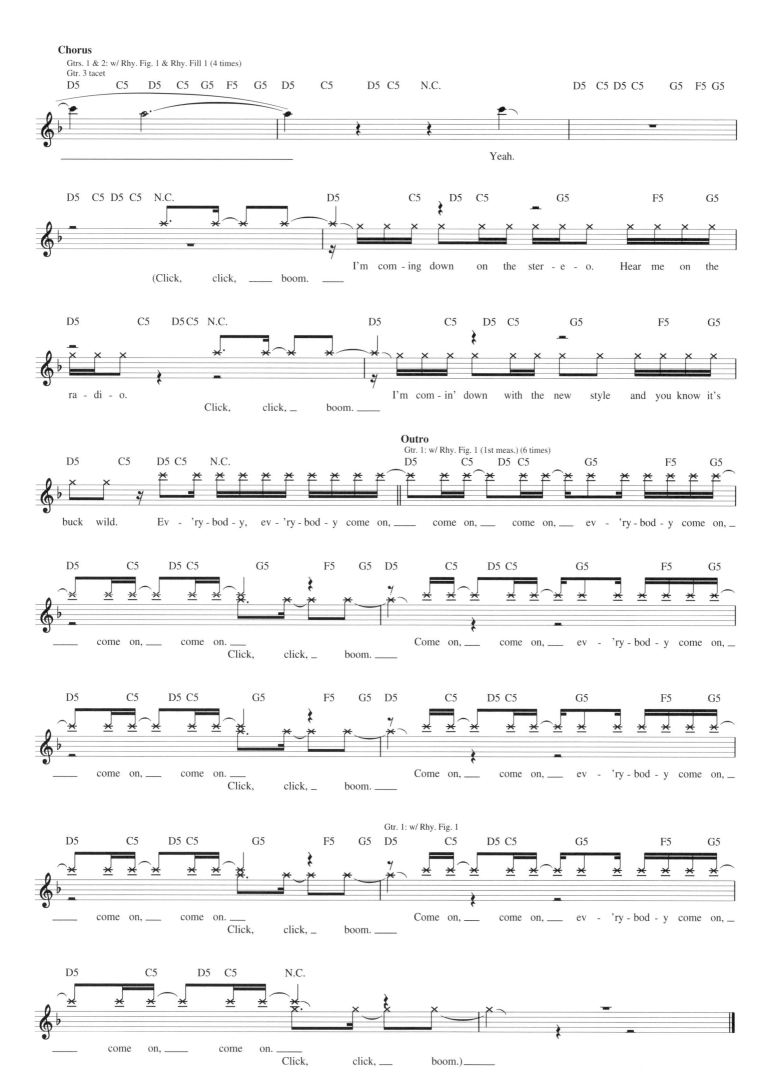

Complicated

Words and Music by Avril Lavigne, Lauren Christy, Scott Spock and Graham Edwards

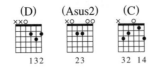

*Two gtrs. arr. for one.

**Chord symbols in parentheses represent chord names respective to detuned guitar.
 Chord symbols above reflect actual sounding chords. Chord symbols reflect overall harmony.
***Two gtrs. arr. for one.

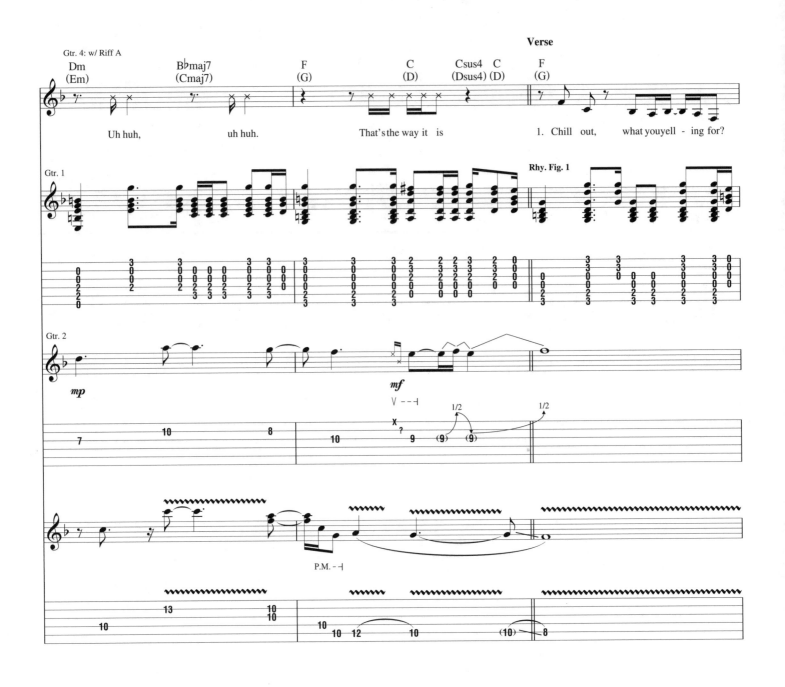

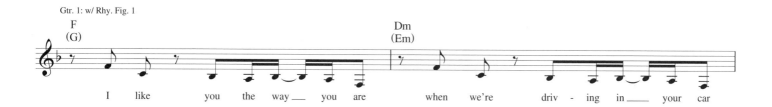

Gtr. 1: w/ Rhy. Fig. 1

F
(G)

I like you the way you are when we're driv-ing in your car

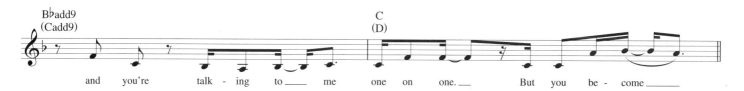

B♭add9
(Cadd9)

C
(D)

and you're talk-ing to me one on one. But you be-come

Pre-Chorus

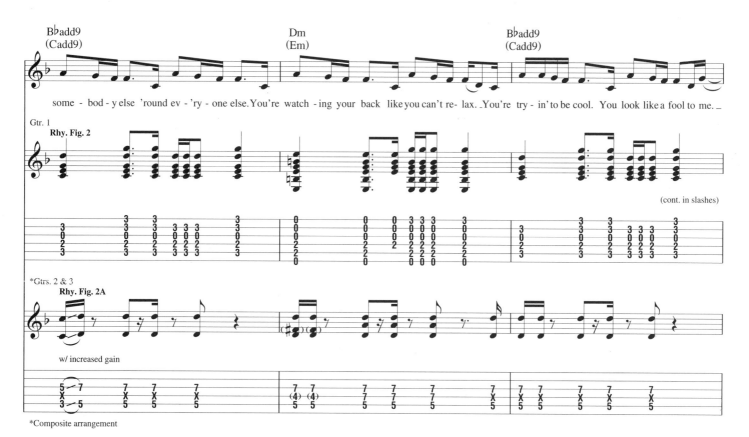

B♭add9
(Cadd9)

Dm
(Em)

B♭add9
(Cadd9)

some-bod-y else 'round ev-'ry-one else. You're watch-ing your back like you can't re-lax. You're try-in' to be cool. You look like a fool to me.

Gtr. 1

Rhy. Fig. 2

(cont. in slashes)

*Gtrs. 2 & 3

Rhy. Fig. 2A

w/ increased gain

*Composite arrangement

Chorus

Gtr. 1 tacet

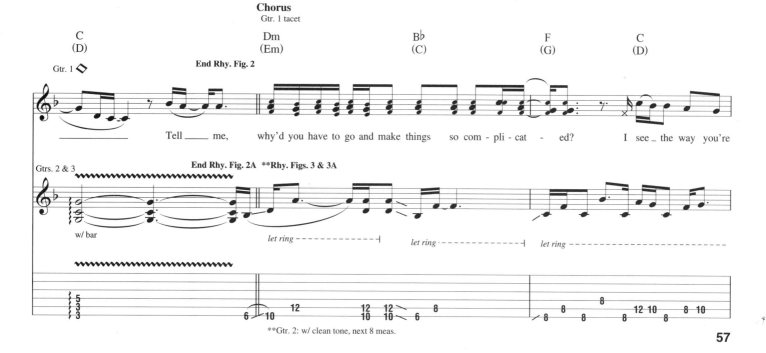

C
(D)

Dm
(Em)

B♭
(C)

F
(G)

C
(D)

Gtr. 1

End Rhy. Fig. 2

Tell me, why'd you have to go and make things so com-pli-cat-ed? I see the way you're

Gtrs. 2 & 3

End Rhy. Fig. 2A **Rhy. Figs. 3 & 3A

w/ bar

let ring

let ring

let ring

**Gtr. 2: w/ clean tone, next 8 meas.

57

act-ing like you're some-bod-y else, __ get-ting me frus-trat - ed. Life's like this, you, __ you fall __ and you crawl __ and you break __ and you take __

let ring sim.

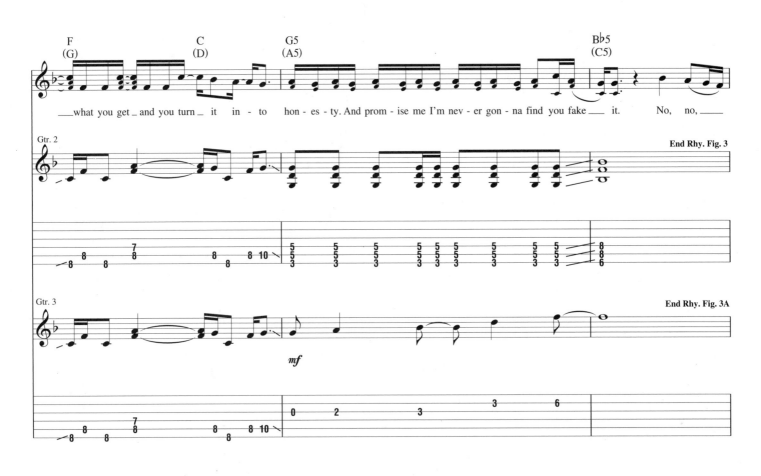

__what you get __ and you turn __ it in - to hon - es - ty. And prom - ise me I'm nev - er gon - na find you fake __ it. No, no, ___

Gtr. 2

End Rhy. Fig. 3

Gtr. 3

End Rhy. Fig. 3A

mf

Verse

Gtrs. 2 & 3 tacet

Gtr. 1: w/ Rhy. Fig. 1 (2 times)

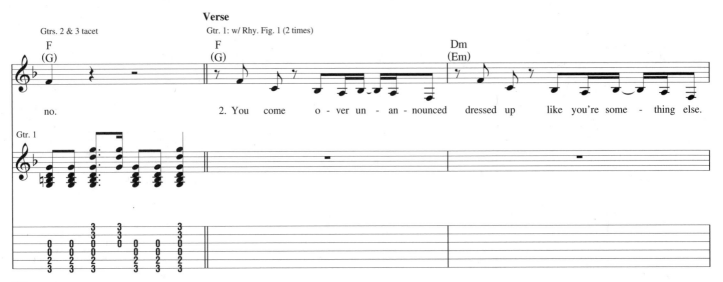

no.   2. You come o - ver un – an - nounced dressed up like you're some - thing else.

Gtr. 1

Where you are ain't where _ it's _ at you see. _ You're mak-ing me _ laugh out when you strike _ a pose.

Gtr. 3

P.M. -

Take off all your prep - py clothes. You know you're not fool - ing an-y-one _ when you be-come

Gtr. 5 (elec.)

mf
w/ dist.
w/ wah-wah as filter
let ring - -

Gtr. 3

P.M. -

Pre-Chorus

Gtrs. 1, 2 & 3: w/ Rhy. Figs. 2 & 2A

some - bod - y else 'round ev - 'ry - one else. You're watch - ing your back like you can't re - lax. You're trying to be cool. You look like a fool to me. _

Gtr. 5

let ring -

**Set tremolo for sextuplet regeneration with multiple repeats.

try - in' to be cool. You look like a fool to me. _____ Tell me, ____

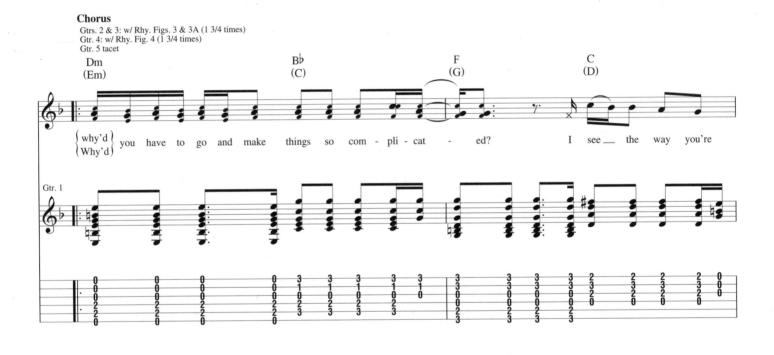

Chorus
Gtrs. 2 & 3: w/ Rhy. Figs. 3 & 3A (1 3/4 times)
Gtr. 4: w/ Rhy. Fig. 4 (1 3/4 times)
Gtr. 5 tacet

{why'd / Why'd} you have to go and make things so com - pli - cat - ed? I see ___ the way you're

Gtr. 1

act - ing like you're some - bod - y else, _ get - ting me frus - trat - ed. Life's like this, you,

you fall__ and you crawl__ and you break__ and you take__ what you get__ and you turn__ it in-to

(2nd time, cont. in slashes)

hon-es-ty. And prom-ise me I'm nev-er gon-na find you fake__ it. No, no.

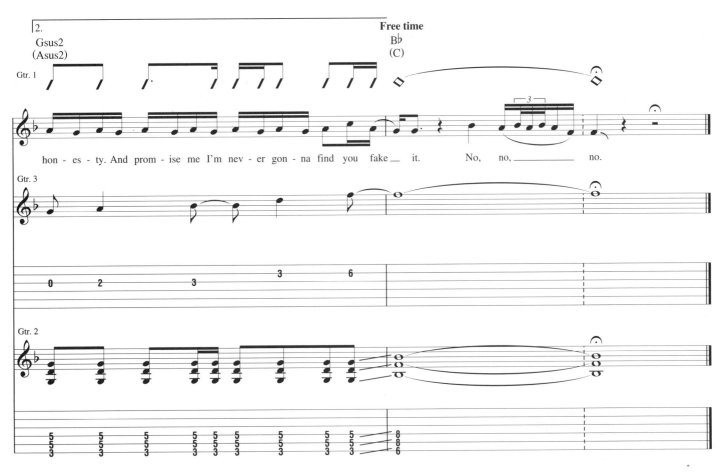

hon-es-ty. And prom-ise me I'm nev-er gon-na find you fake__ it. No, no,_____ no,

Control

Words and Music by Brad Stewart and Wesley Reid Scantlin

Verse

Gtr. 1 tacet
2nd time, Gtr. 3 tacet

way __ you look __ at me, _____ I feel the pain you place __ in - side. __ You lock me
way __ you rake my skin, _____ I feel the hate you place __ in - side. __ I need to

* Chord symbols reflect implied harmony.

up in - side __ your dir - ty ____ cage, __ well, I'm a - lone in - side __ my mind. __ I like to
get your voice __ out of my __ head, __ 'cause I'm that guy you'll nev - er find. __ I think you

teach you all __ the rules, _____ I get to see them set __ in stone. __ I like it
know all of __ the rules, _____ there's no ex - pres - sions on __ your face. __ I hope that

* w/ delay

* Set delay for eighth-note regeneration with 3 repeats.

when you chain __ me to the bed, __ but then your se - crets nev - er show. _____
some - day you __ will let me go, _____ re - lease me from __ my dir - ty cage.

delay off   *w/ dist.*

w/ wah-wah

𝄋 Chorus

I _____ need __ to feel __ you, you _____ need __ to feel __ me.

Gtrs. 1 & 2

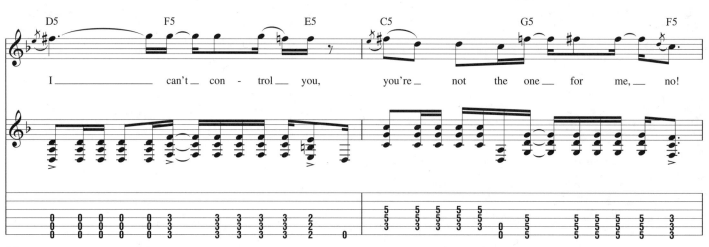

I _____ can't con - trol __ you, you're __ not the one __ for me, __ no!

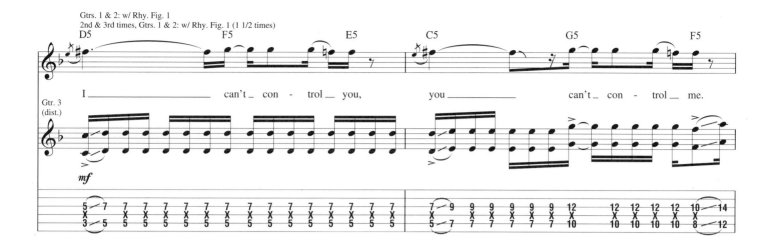

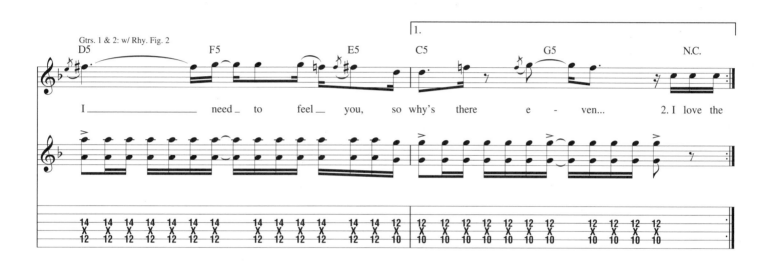

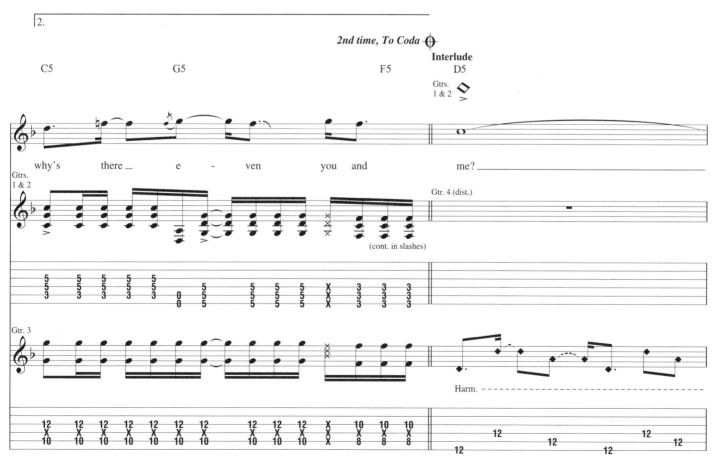

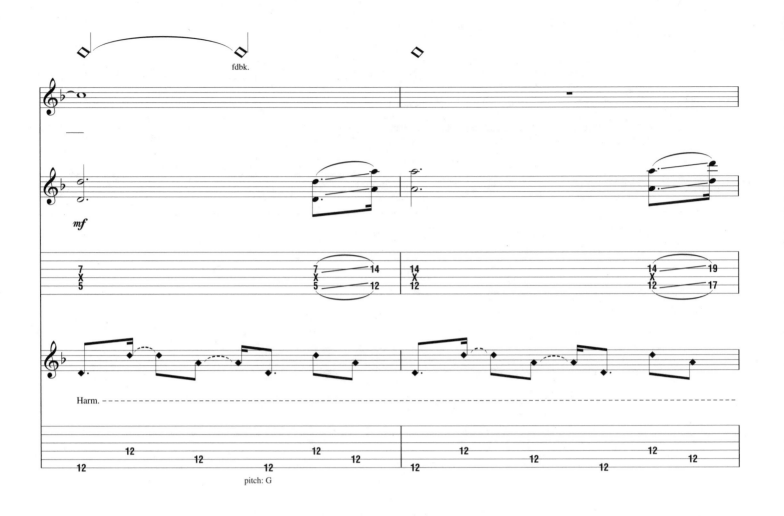

pitch: G

Bridge
Gtrs. 3 & 4 tacet
C5   D5   C5   D5   F5

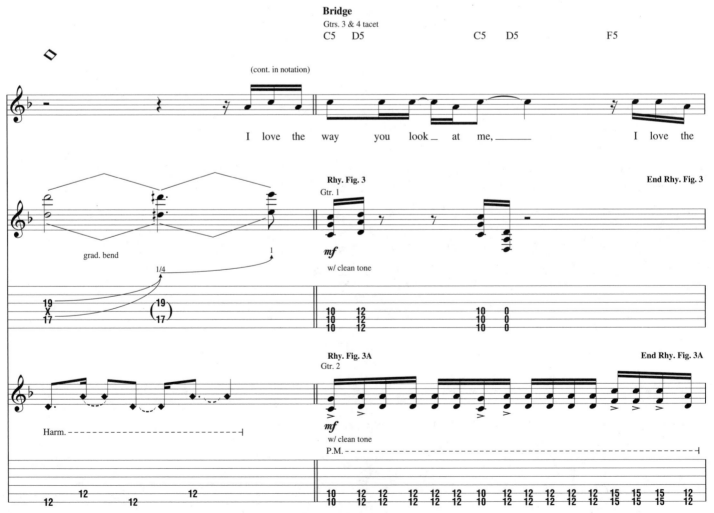

I love the way you look__ at me,_____   I love the

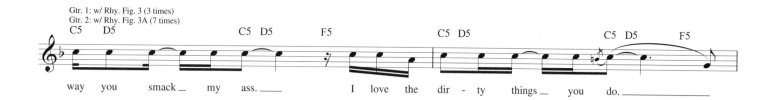

way you smack my ass. I love the dirty things you do.

I have control of you. I love the way you look at me, I love the

*pitch: G   *f, w/ dist.

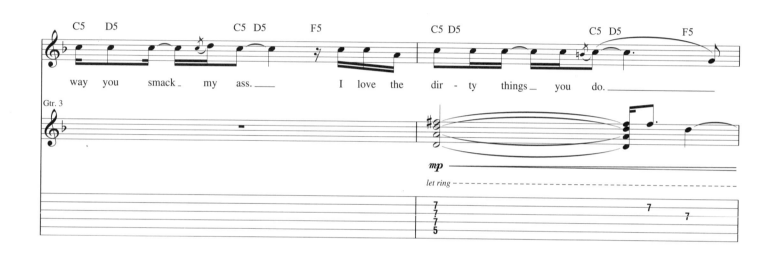

way you smack my ass. I love the dirty things you do.

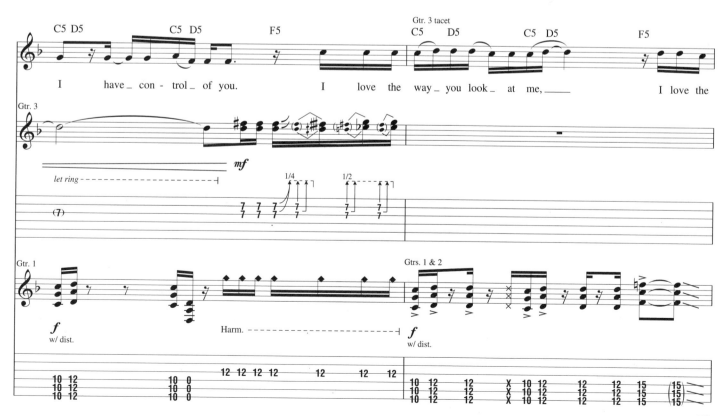

I have control of you. I love the way you look at me, I love the

D.S. al Coda
(take 2nd ending)

⊕ **Coda**
Outro
Gtrs. 1 & 2: w/ Rhy. Fig. 1 (3 1/2 times)
Gtr. 3: w/ Riff A

Riff B
Gtr. 4   *8va* -

* w/ chorus, phase & delay

* Set delay for eighth-note regeneration
  with multiple repeats.

Downfall

Words and Music by James Fukai, Joshua Moates, Kevin Palmer and Jason Singleton

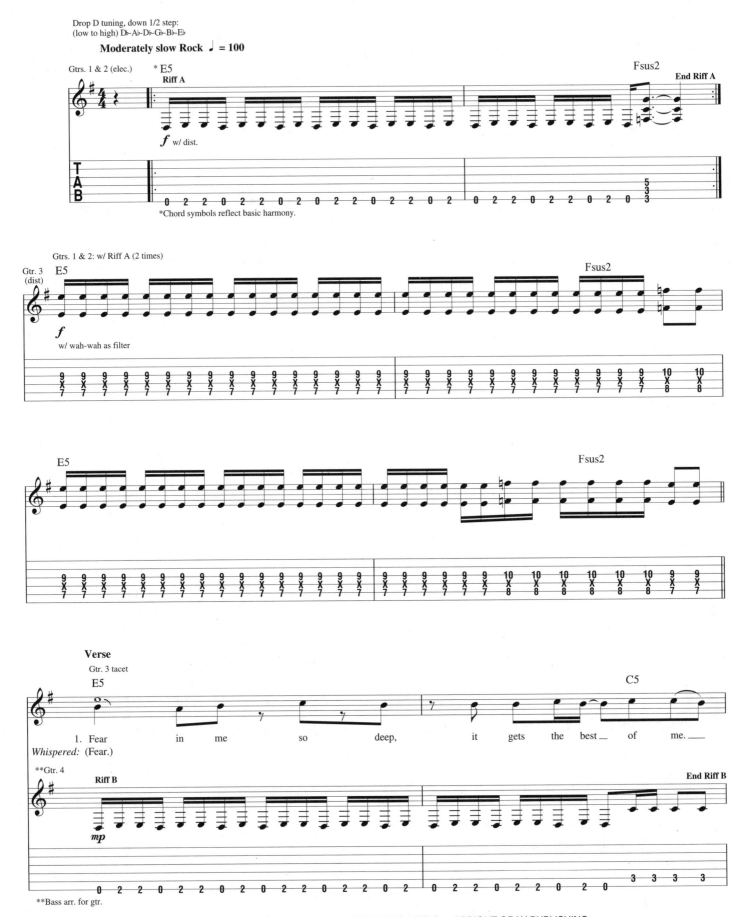

Gtr. 4: w/ Riff B (3 times)

E5   C5   E5   C5

In the fear I fall. Here it comes, face to face _ with me. __ Here I stand, hold back so no one can see. _
Whispered: (Here.)

Pre-Chorus

Gtrs. 1 & 2: w/ Riff A

E5   C5   E5   Fsus2

__ I feel these wounds. Step down... Step down... Step. Oh! __ Am I break - ing?

%. **Chorus**

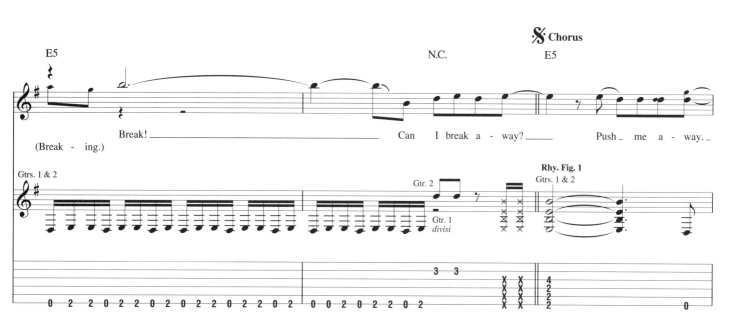

E5   N.C.   E5

Break! __ Can I break a - way? __ Push _ me a - way. _
(Break - ing.)

Gtrs. 1 & 2

Gtr. 2

Gtr. 1
divisi

Rhy. Fig. 1
Gtrs. 1 & 2

C5   G5 Gsus2   D5

__ Make __ me fall __ just __ to _ see _ an - oth - er side _ of me. _

End Rhy. Fig. 1

To Coda

Gtrs. 1 & 2: w/ Rhy. Fig. 1

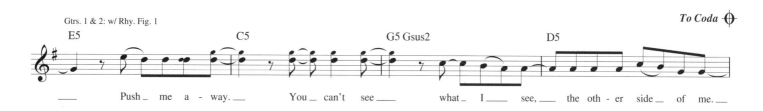

E5   C5   G5 Gsus2   D5

__ Push _ me a - way. _ You _ can't see what _ I _ see, _ the oth - er side _ of me. _

73

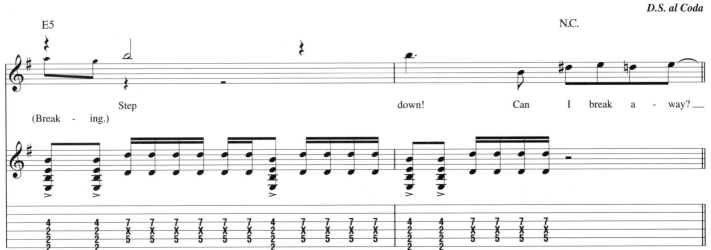

Coda

Interlude
Gtr. 3 tacet

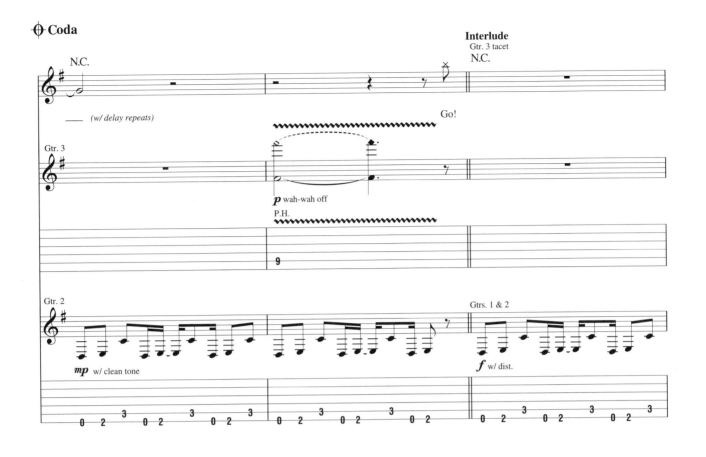

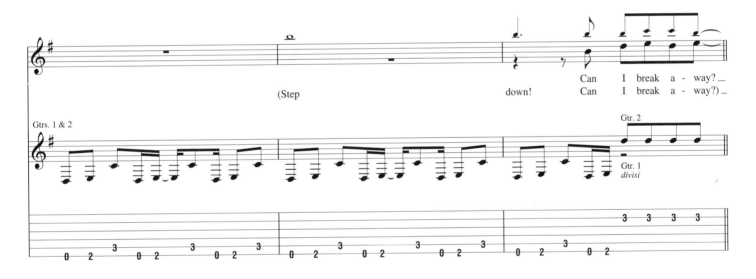

75

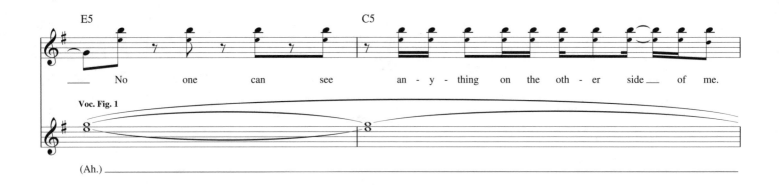

No one can see an-y-thing on the oth-er side ___ of me.

Voc. Fig. 1

(Ah.) _____

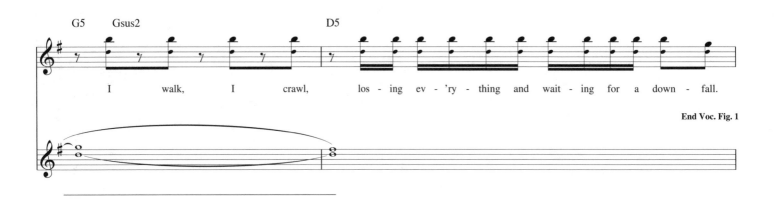

I walk, I crawl, los-ing ev-'ry-thing and wait-ing for a down-fall.

End Voc. Fig. 1

Bkgd. Voc.: w/ Voc. Fig. 1

No one can see an-y-thing on the oth-er side ___ of me. I walk, I crawl,

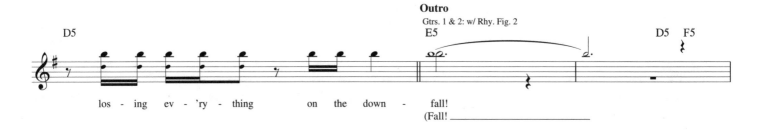

Outro

Gtrs. 1 & 2: w/ Rhy. Fig. 2

los-ing ev-'ry-thing on the down-fall!

(Fall! _____

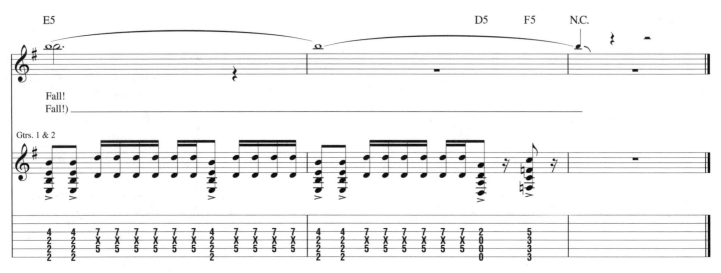

Fall!
Fall!) _____

Gtrs. 1 & 2

Drive

Words and Music by Brandon Boyd, Michael Einziger, Alex Katunich, Jose Pasillas II and Chris Kilmore

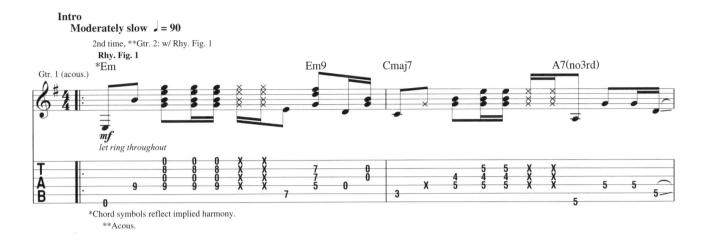

Intro
Moderately slow ♩ = 90

2nd time, **Gtr. 2: w/ Rhy. Fig. 1

*Chord symbols reflect implied harmony.
**Acous.

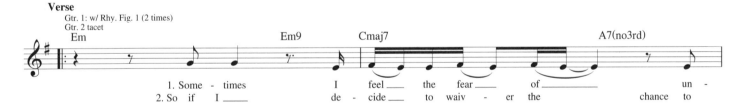

Verse
Gtr. 1: w/ Rhy. Fig. 1 (2 times)
Gtr. 2 tacet

1. Some - times   I feel ___ the fear ___ of ___   un -
2. So if I ___   de - cide ___ to waiv - er the   chance to

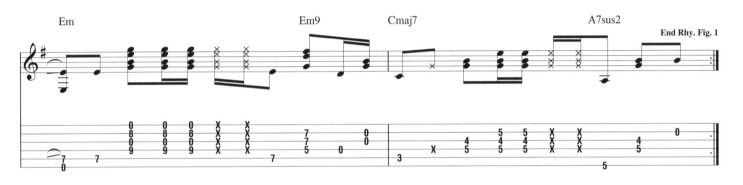

cer - tain - ty ___   sting - ing   clear. ___   And I, ___   I can't
be one of ___   the   hive, _   will I ___   choose

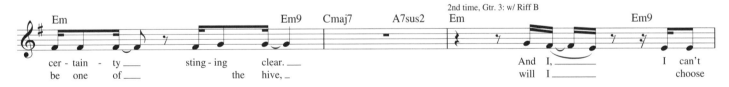

help but ask my - self how much I'll let the fear ___   take the wheel ___ and ___ steer.
wa - ter o - ver wine and hold my own and drive? ___   Oh, _____   oh,   oh.

Riff B
Gtr. 3

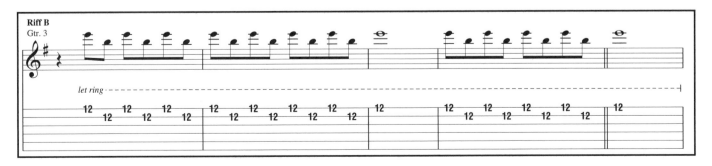

let ring - - - - - - - - - - - - - - - - -

*Composite arrangement

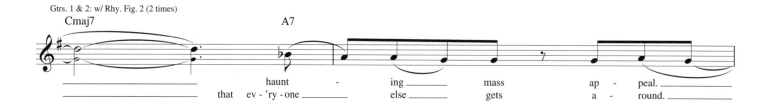

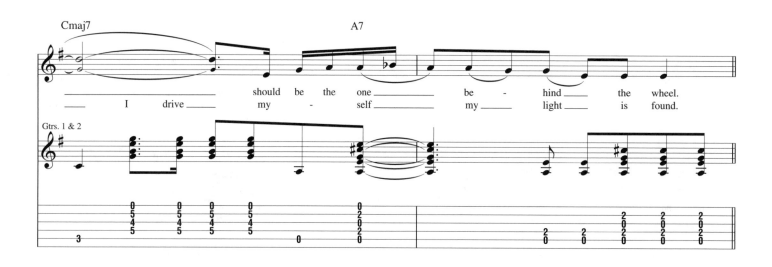

Chorus

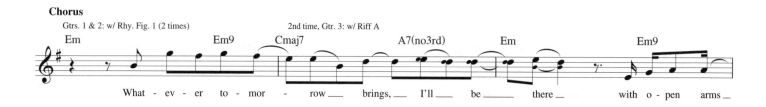

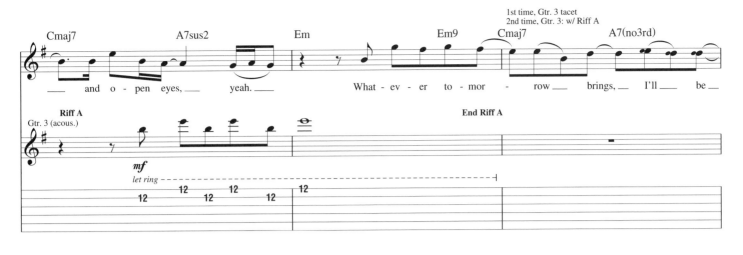

Interlude

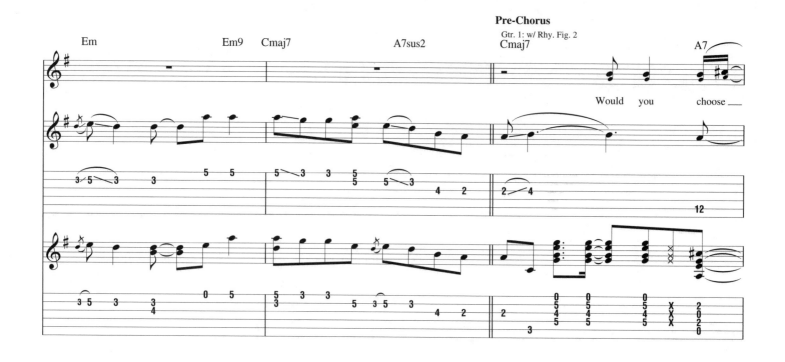

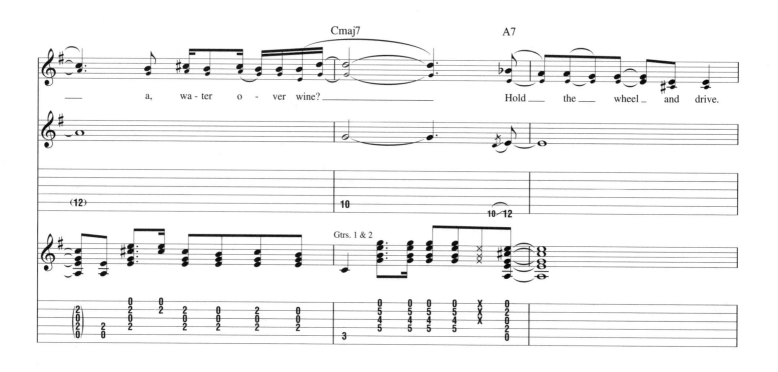

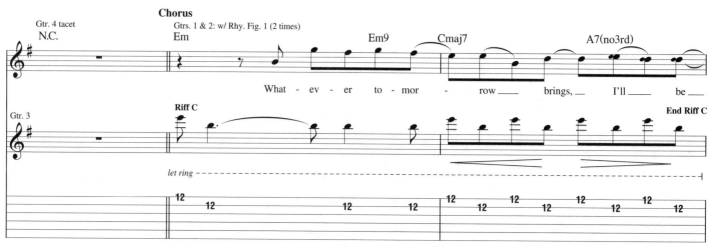

Gtr. 3: w/ Riff C (3 times)

there _with o - pen arms_ _and o - pen eyes,_ _yeah._ What - ev - er to - mor -

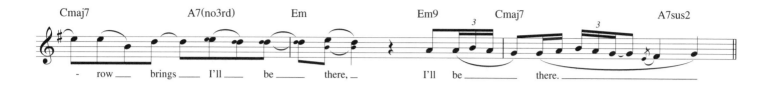

- row _brings_ _I'll_ _be_ _there,_ I'll be _there._

Outro

Gtrs. 1 & 2: w/ Rhy. Fig. 1 (2 times)
Gtr. 3: w/ Riff C (3 times)

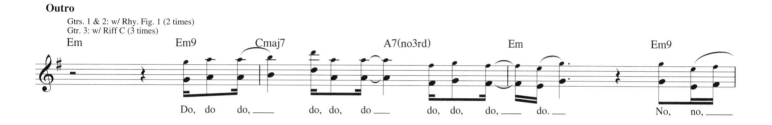

Do, do do, _____ do, do, do _____ do, do, do, _____ do. No, no, _____

Gtr. 5 tacet

Gtr. 5: w/ Riff D

_____ no. Do, do, do, _ do, do. _____ Do, do, do, do, _____ do, do, do, _____ do, do, do, _

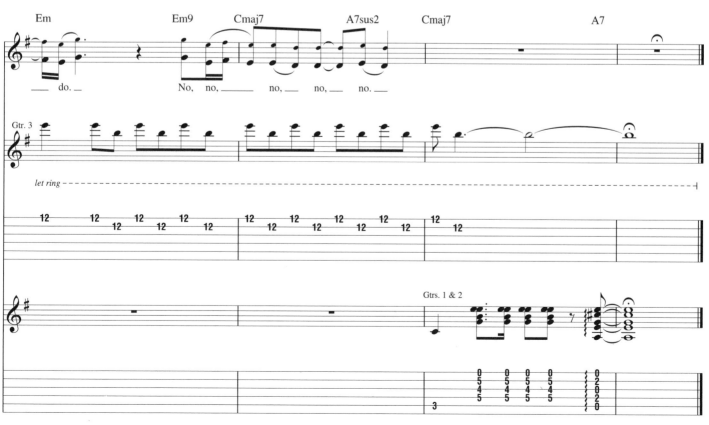

_____ do. No, no, _____ no, _ no, _ no. _____

let ring

Gtr. 3

Gtrs. 1 & 2

Fat Lip

Words and Music by Sum 41

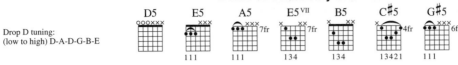

Drop D tuning:
(low to high) D-A-D-G-B-E

D5   E5   A5   E5 VII   B5   C#5   G#5

Intro

Moderately slow Rock ♩ = 100

Verse

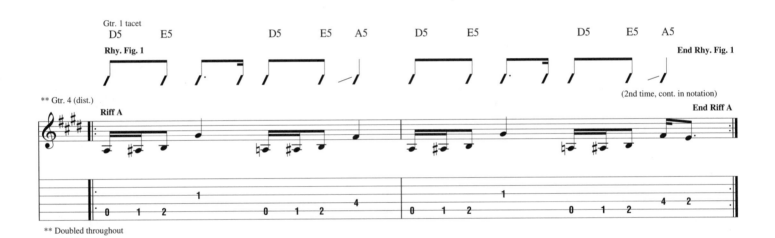

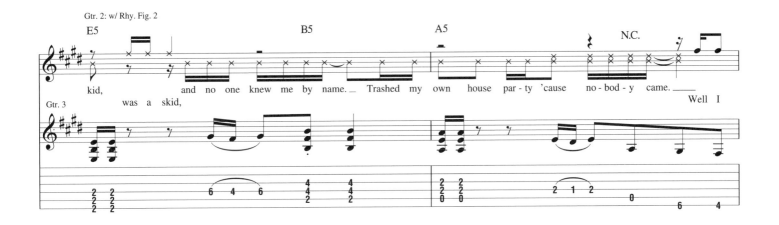

kid, and no one knew me by name.___ Trashed my own house par-ty 'cause no-bod-y came.___ Well I was a skid,

Pre-Chorus
Double-time feel

know I'm not the one you thought you knew back in high___ school, nev-er go-ing, nev-er show-ing up when we had___ to. (Is it) at-

2. See additional lyrics

-ten-tion that we crave? Don't tell us to be-have. I'm sick of al-ways hear-ing "Act your age". I don't want to

Chorus

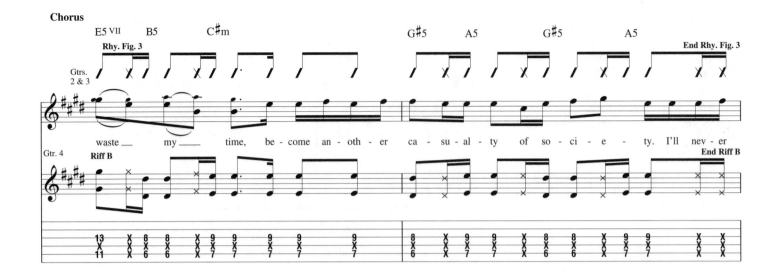

waste my time, be-come an-oth-er ca-su-al-ty of so-ci-e-ty. I'll nev-er

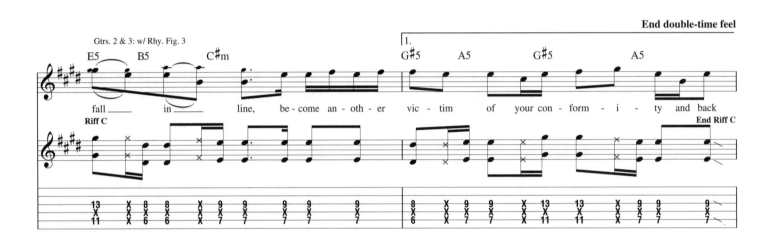

fall in line, be-come an-oth-er vic-tim of your con-form-i-ty and back

Interlude

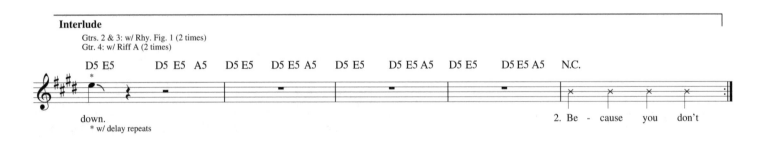

down.
* w/ delay repeats

2. Be-cause you don't

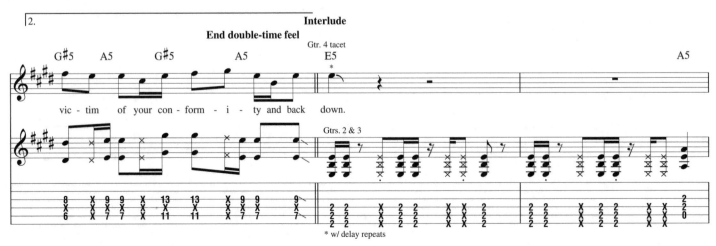

vic-tim of your con-form-i-ty and back down.

* w/ delay repeats

84

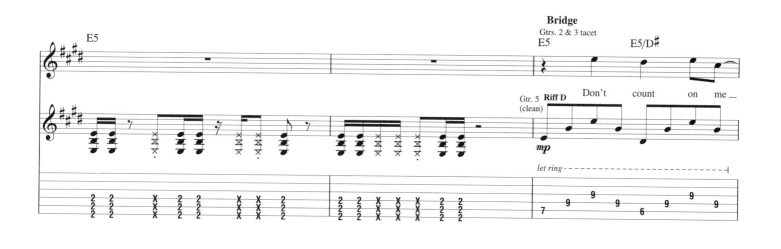

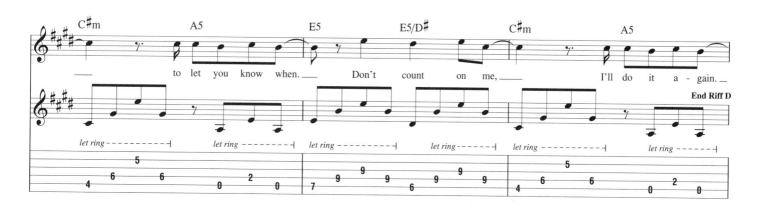

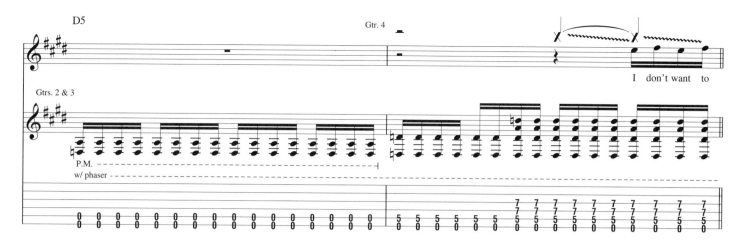

I don't want to

Chorus
Double-time feel

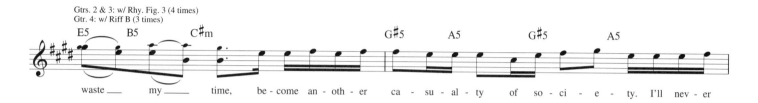

waste __ my __ time, be - come an - oth - er ca - su - al - ty of so - ci - e - ty. I'll nev - er

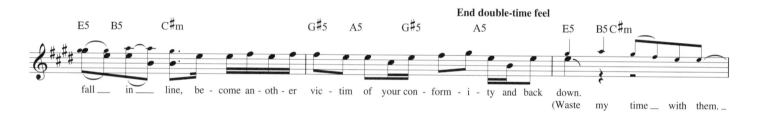

fall __ in __ line, be - come an - oth - er vic - tim of your con - form - i - ty and back down.
(Waste my time __ with them. __

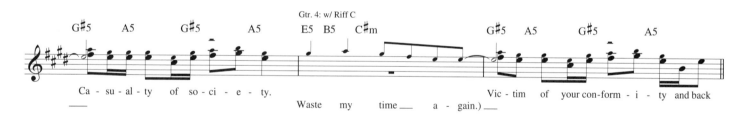

__ Ca - su - al - ty of so - ci - e - ty. Waste my time __ a - gain.) Vic - tim of your con - form - i - ty and back

Outro

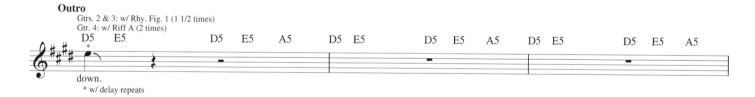

down.

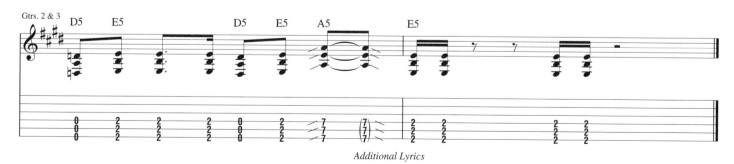

Additional Lyrics

2. Because you don't
Know us at all, we laugh when old people fall.
But what would you expect with a conscience so small?
Heavy Metal and mullets, it's how we were raised.
Maiden and Priest were gods that we praised.

2nd Pre-Chorus:
'Cause we like having fun at other people's expense and
Cutting people down is just a minor offense then.
It's none of your concern, I guess I'll never learn.
I'm sick of being told to wait my turn.
I don't want to...

The Game of Love

Words and Music by Rick Nowels and Gregg Alexander

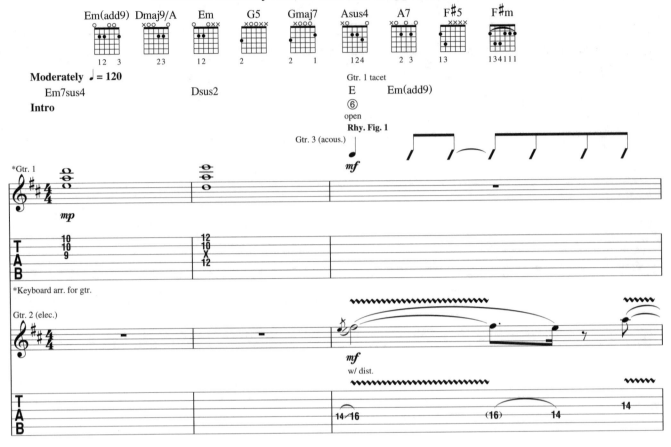

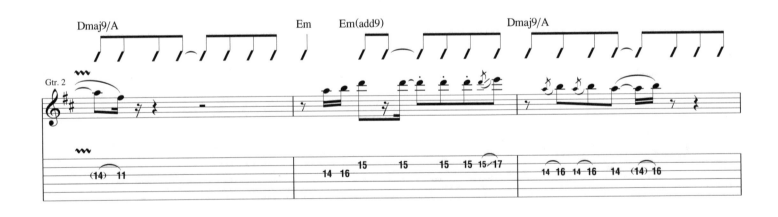

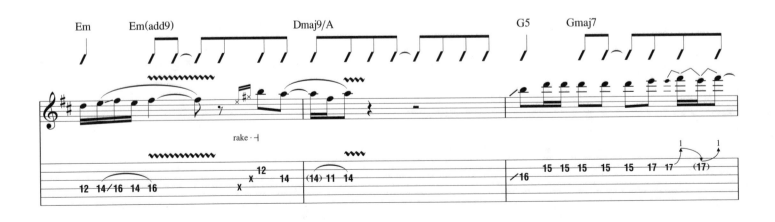

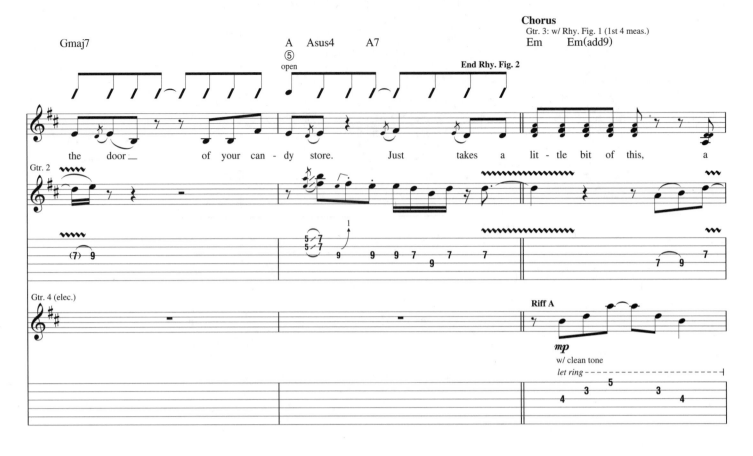

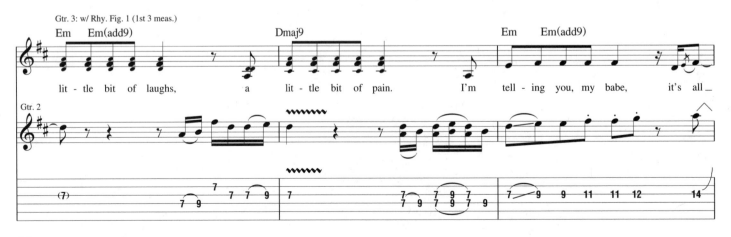

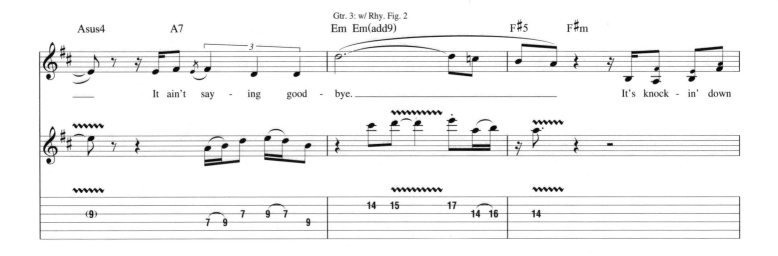

It ain't say - ing good - bye. _____ It's knock - in' down

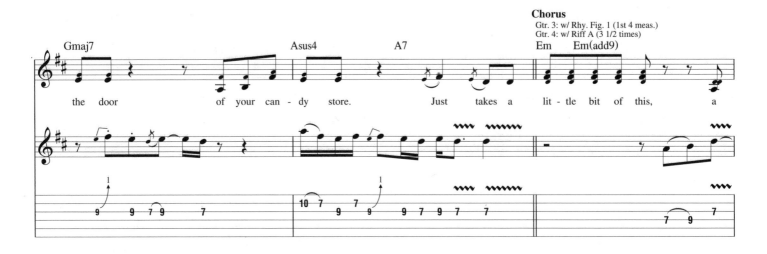

Chorus
Gtr. 3: w/ Rhy. Fig. 1 (1st 4 meas.)
Gtr. 4: w/ Riff A (3 1/2 times)

the door of your can - dy store. Just takes a lit - tle bit of this, a

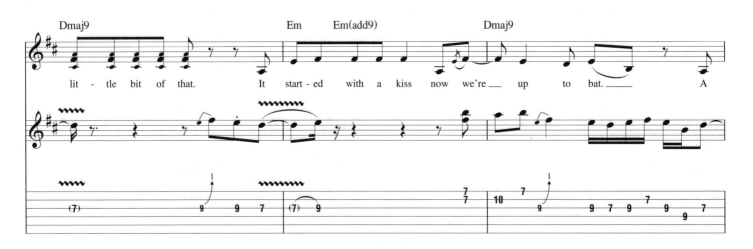

lit - tle bit of that. It start - ed with a kiss now we're __ up to bat. __ A

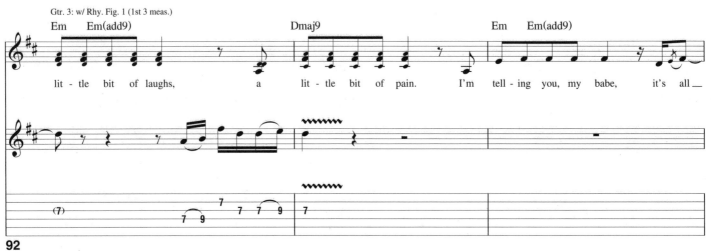

lit - tle bit of laughs, a lit - tle bit of pain. I'm tell - ing you, my babe, it's all __

92

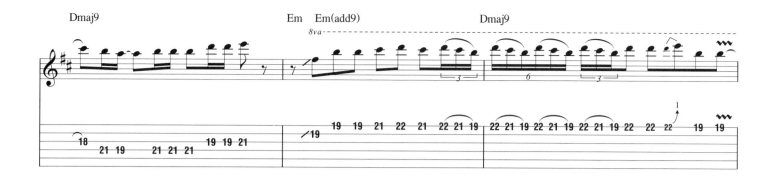

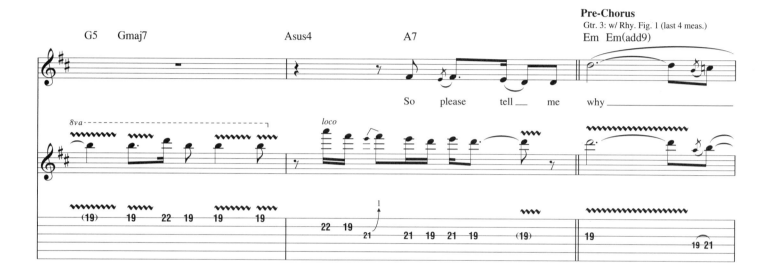

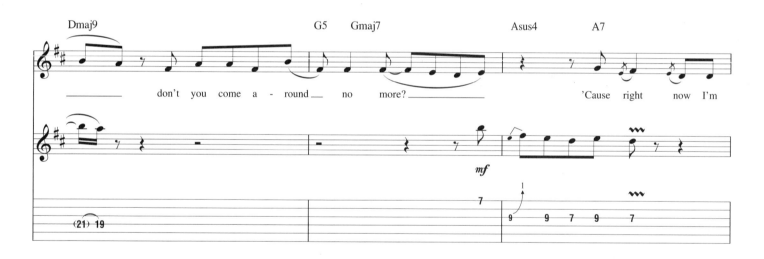

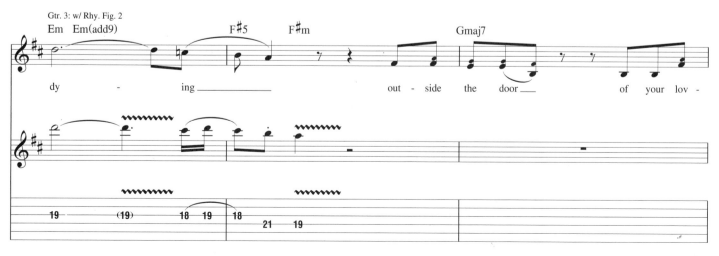

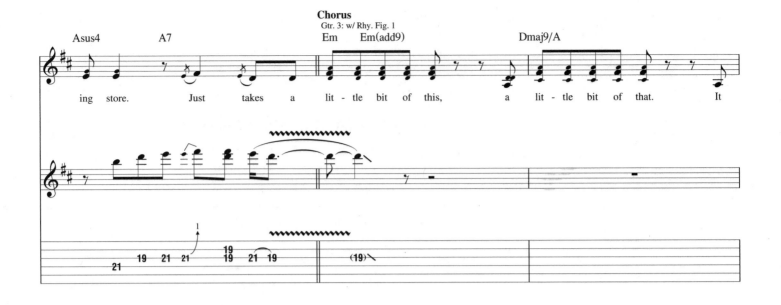

Outro-Chorus

Gtr. 3: w/ Rhy. Fig. 1 (till fade)
Gtr. 4: w/ Riff A (3 1/2 times)

It's all ___ in this game ___ of love. ___ It's all ___

Voc. Fig. 1

lit - tle bit of this, a lit - tle bit of that.

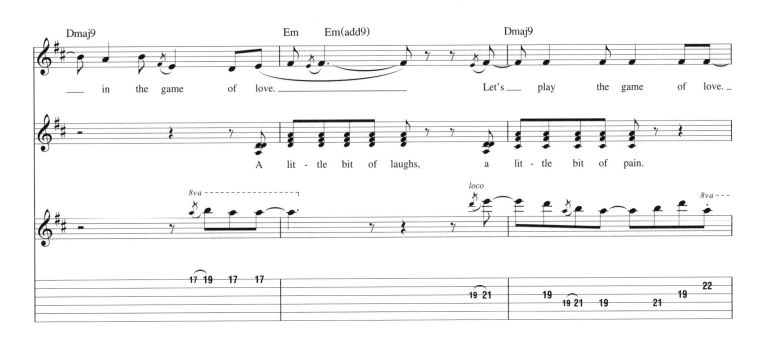

___ in the game of love. ___ Let's ___ play the game of love. ___

A lit - tle bit of laughs, a lit - tle bit of pain.

Gtr. 4: w/ Fill 1

Bkgd. Voc.: w/ Voc. Fig. 1 (till fade)
Gtr. 4: w/ Riff A (3 1/2 times)

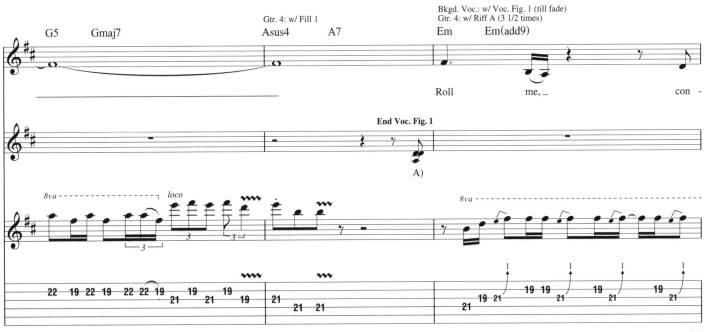

Roll me, ___ con -

End Voc. Fig. 1

A)

Get Free

Words and Music by Craig Nicholls

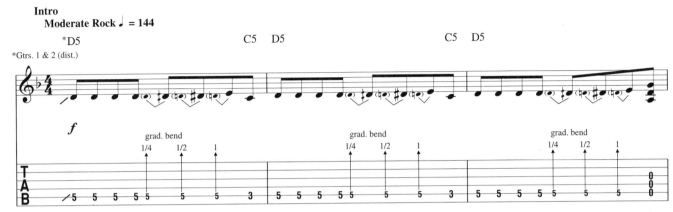

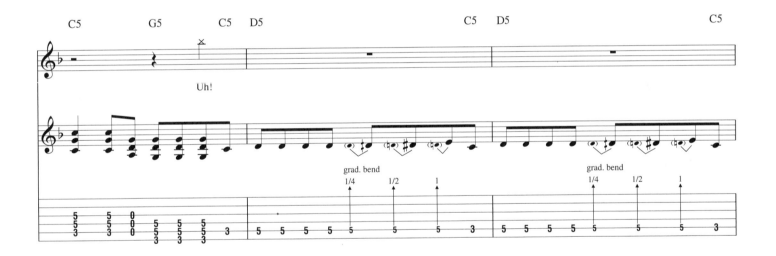

Interlude

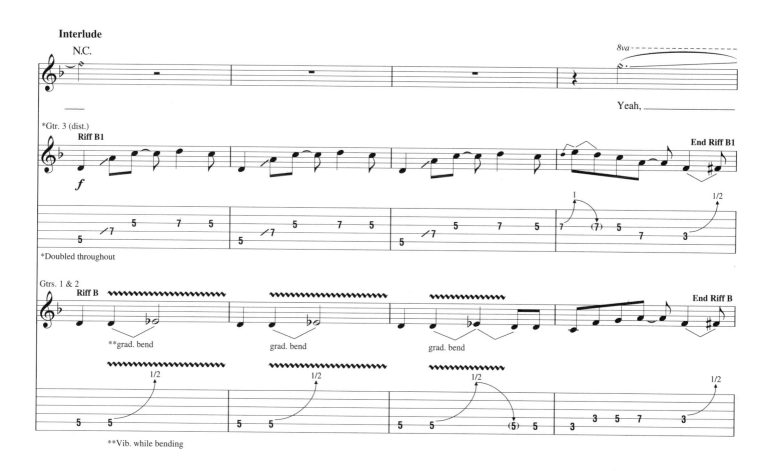

Gtr. 3 (dist.)

Riff B1

End Riff B1

*Doubled throughout

Gtrs. 1 & 2

Riff B

End Riff B

**grad. bend

grad. bend

grad. bend

**Vib. while bending

Gtrs. 1, 2 & 3: w/ Riffs B & B1

ah,   oo! _____

Verse

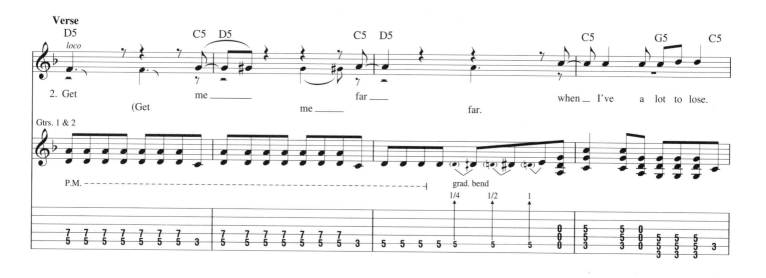

2. Get   me ____ far ____   when __ I've   a lot to lose.
(Get   me ____   far.

Gtrs. 1 & 2

P.M. --

grad. bend

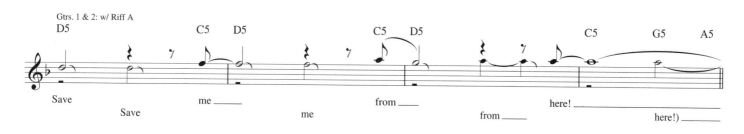

Gtrs. 1 & 2: w/ Riff A

Save   me ____   from ____   here! ____
Save   me   from ____   here!) ____

Bkgd. Voc.: w/ Voc. Fig. 1
Gtrs. 1 & 2: w/ Rhy. Fig. 1 (3 1/2 times)

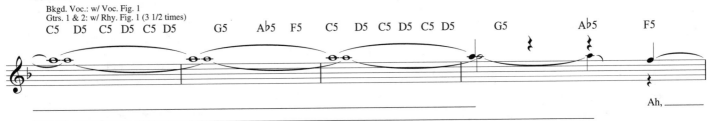

C5 D5 C5 D5 C5 D5　　　G5　　Ab5　F5　C5 D5 C5 D5 C5 D5　　　G5　　　Ab5　　F5

Ah,

C5 D5 C5 D5 C5 D5　　　G5　　　Ab5　　F5　　C5　D5　　C5 D5　　C5　　D5

uh,　　　huh.

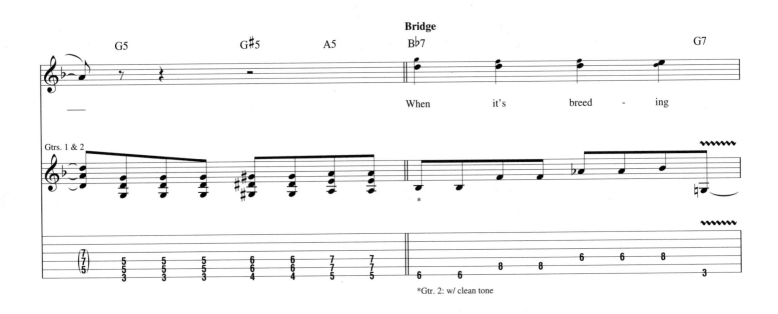

G5　　　　G#5　　A5　　**Bridge** Bb7　　　　　　　　　　G7

When　　it's　　breed　-　ing

Gtrs. 1 & 2

*Gtr. 2: w/ clean tone

Bb7　　　　　　　　　　　　　　　　　　　A7

time, _____　　look　in - to　your

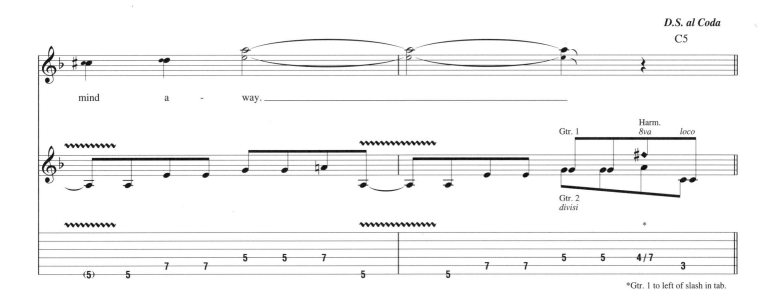

mind   a -   way. _____

*Gtr. 1 to left of slash in tab.

⊕ Coda

Free time

**Pick behind nut.

Heaven

Words and Music by Henry Garza, Joey Garza and Ringo Garza

Tune down 1/2 step:
(low to high) E♭-A♭-D♭-G♭-B♭-E♭

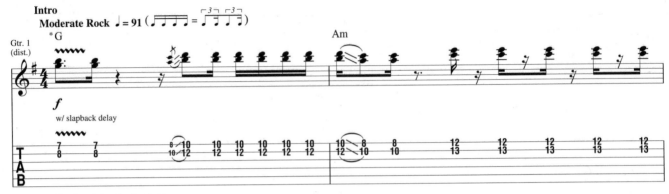

*Chord symbols reflect implied harmony.

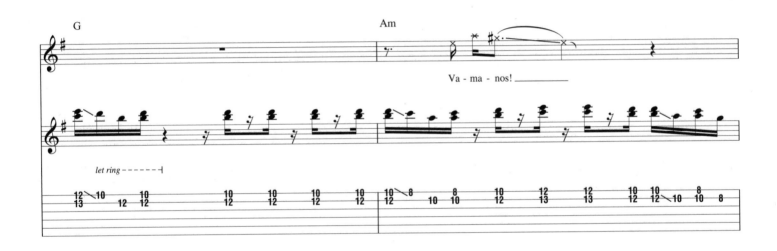

Va - ma - nos!

let ring - - - - - -

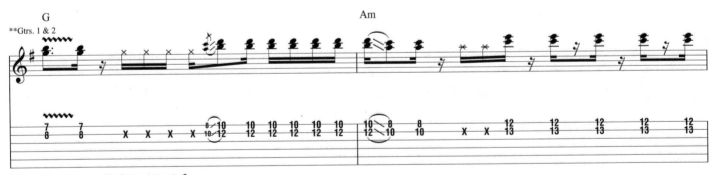

**Composite arrangement, Gtr. 2 (clean) played *mf*.

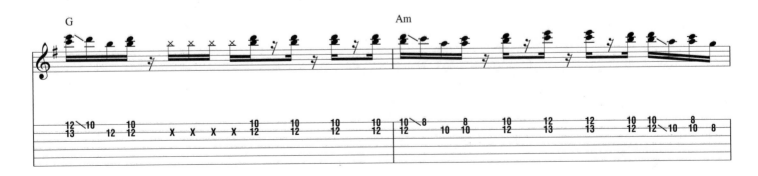

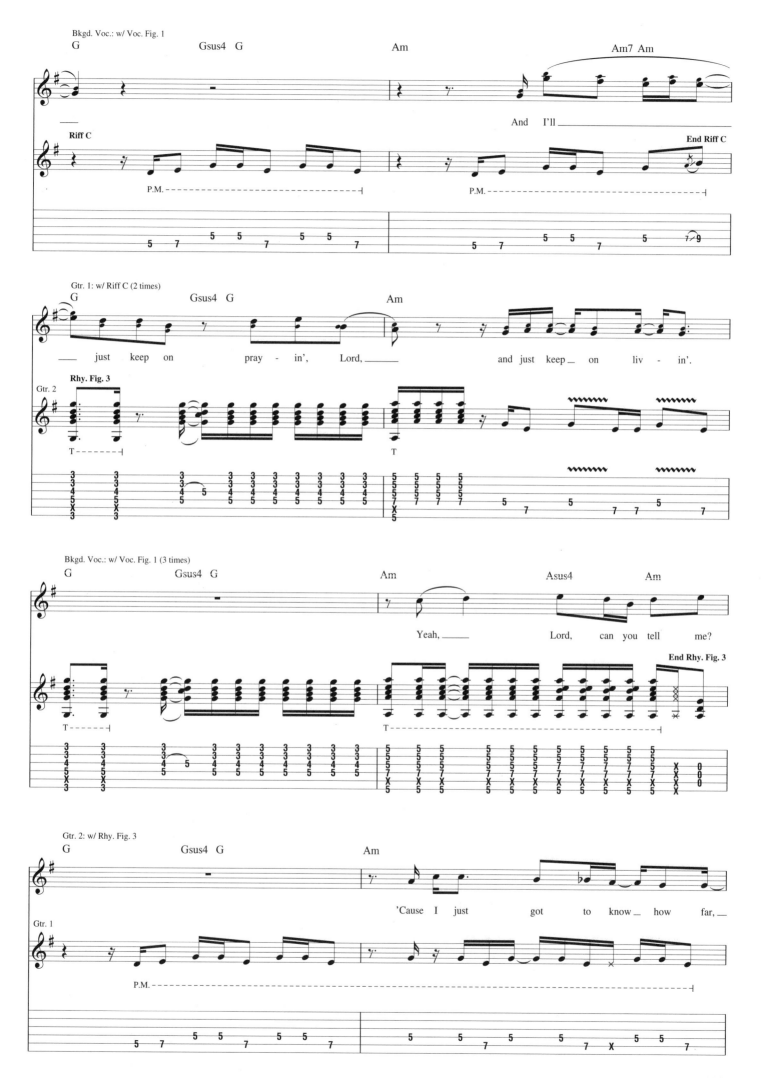

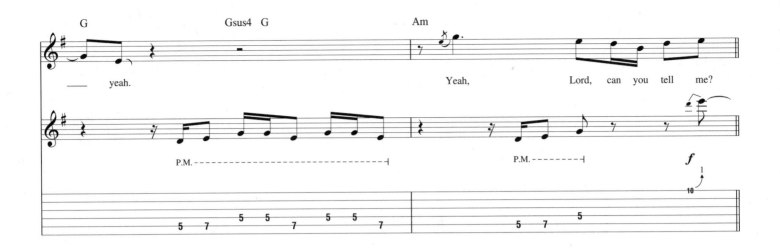

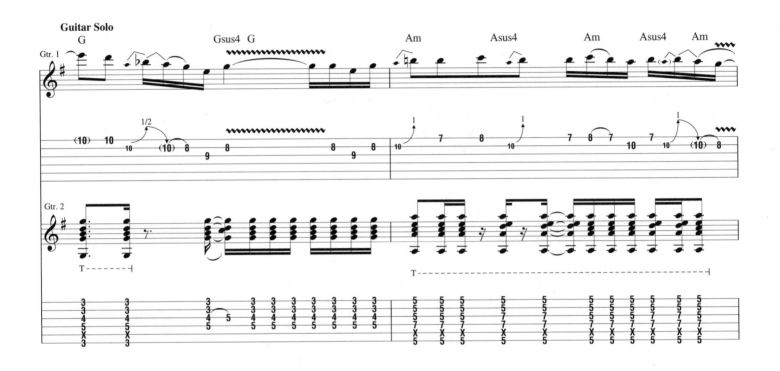

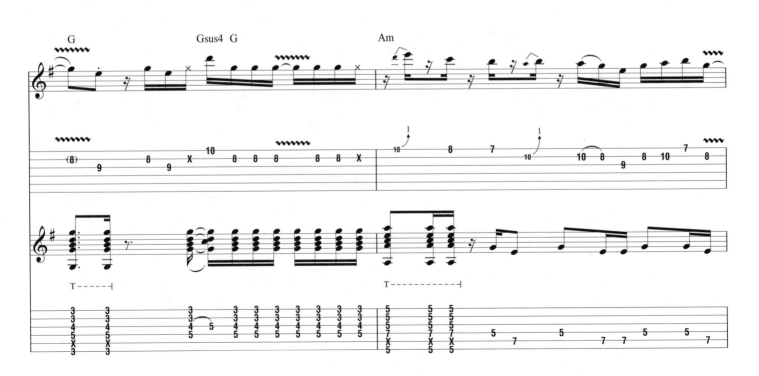

Tú que es - tás____ en - trad - - o al ci - el - o,____

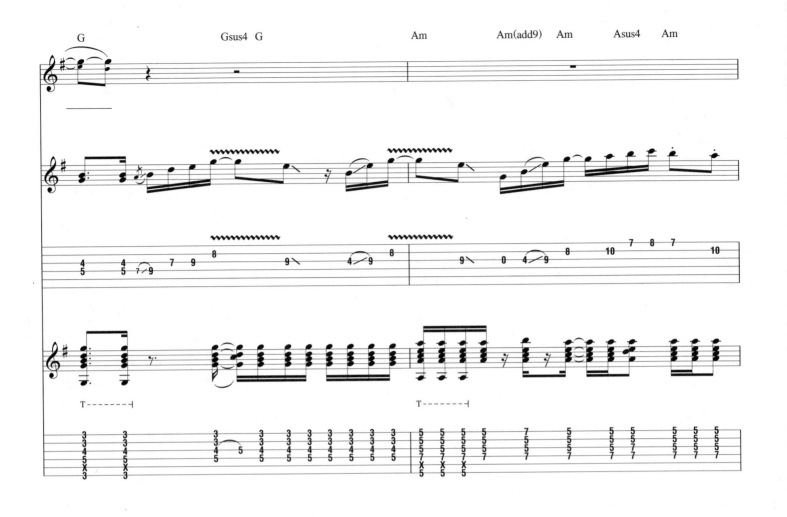

Gtr. 2: w/ Rhy. Fig. 3 (till fade)

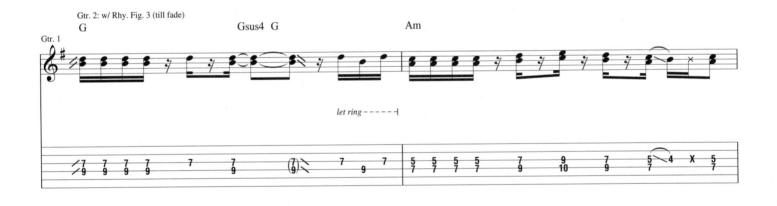

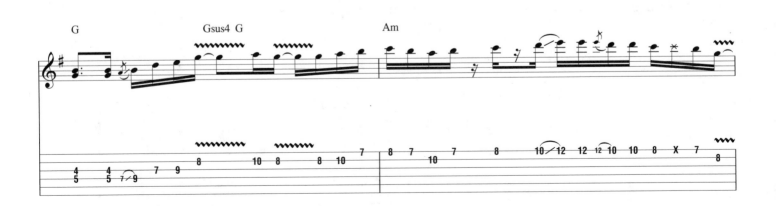

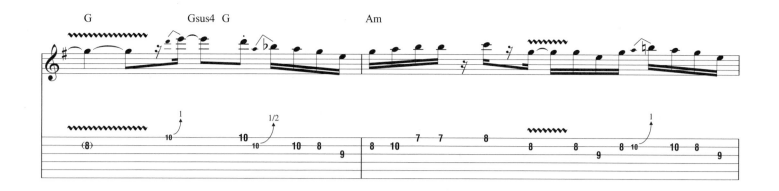

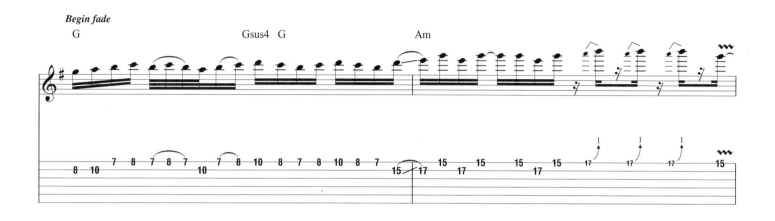

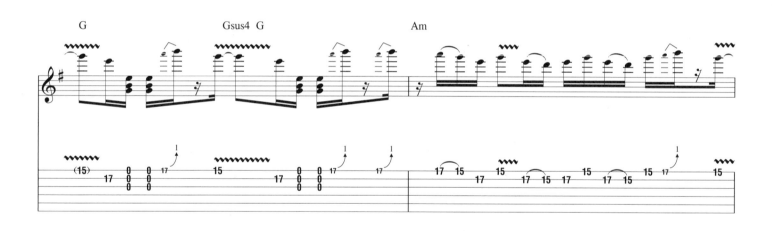

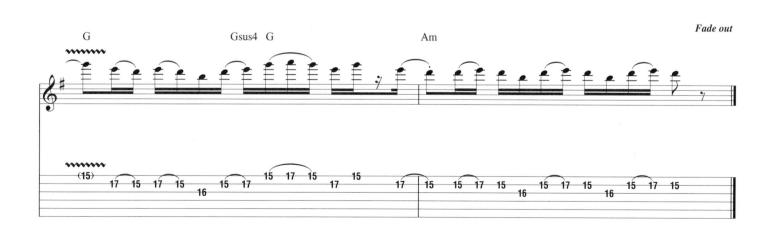

If You're Gone

Written by Rob Thomas

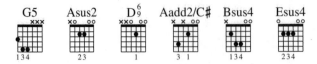

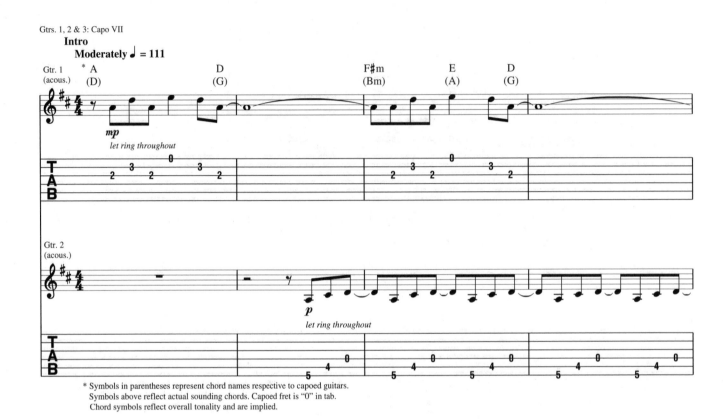

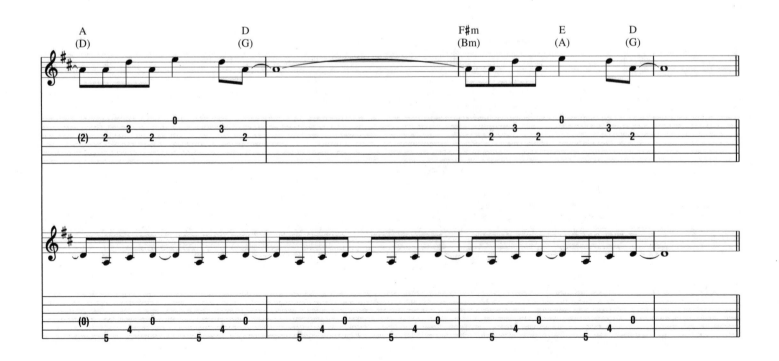

* Symbols in parentheses represent chord names respective to capoed guitars.
Symbols above reflect actual sounding chords. Capoed fret is "0" in tab.
Chord symbols reflect overall tonality and are implied.

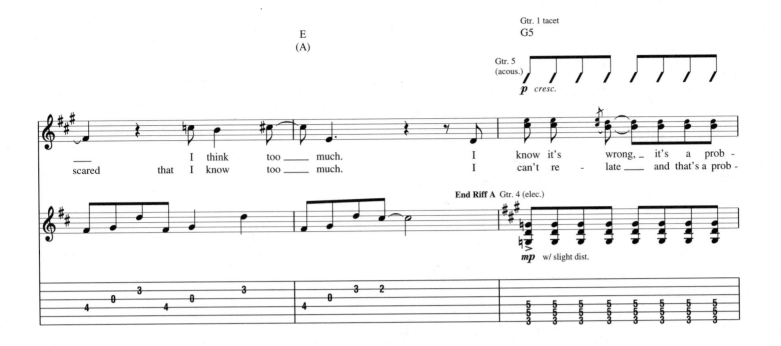

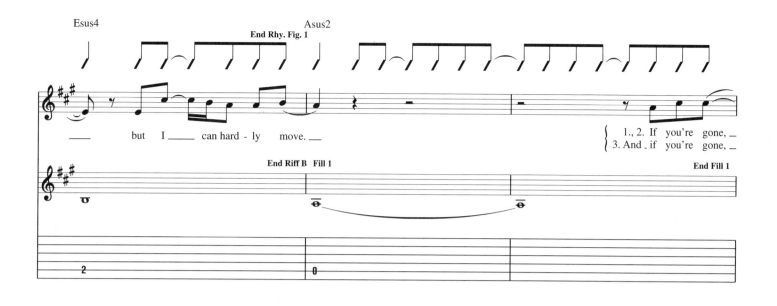

but I ___ can hard - ly move. ___

1., 2. If you're gone, ___
3. And _ if you're gone, ___

ba - by, you need ___ to come home, ___
yeah, ba - by, you need ___ to come home, ___

come ___

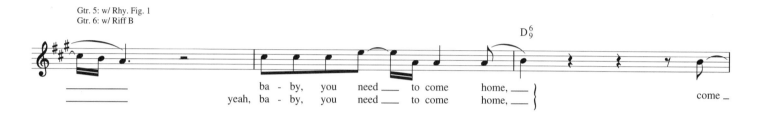

To Coda 1 ⊕   *To Coda 2* ⊕

___ home. There's a lit - tle bit of some-thing me ___

in ev - 'ry-thing in ___

D.S. al Coda 1
(take 2nd ending)

Interlude

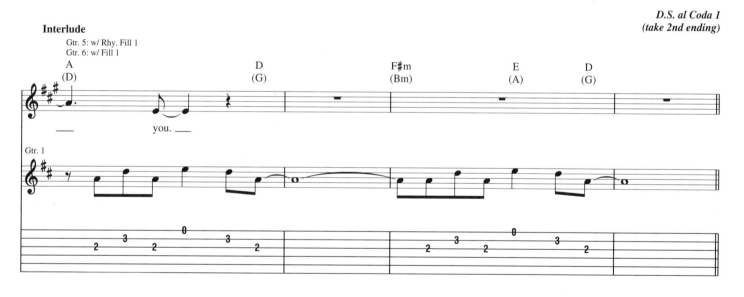

you. ___

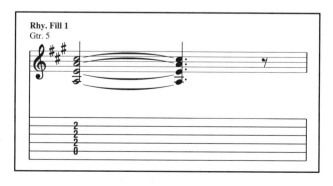

Coda 2

Outro

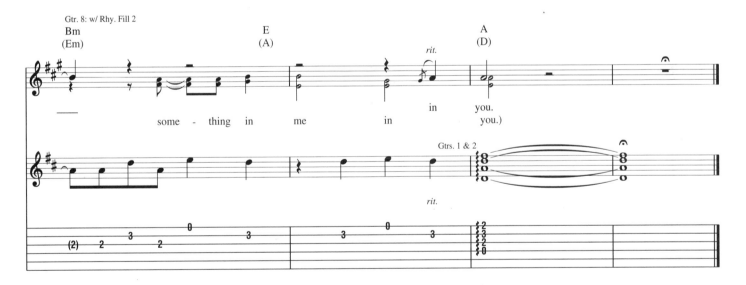

Just Because

Words and Music by Perry Farrell, Dave Navarro, Stephen Perkins, Bob Ezrin and Christopher Chaney

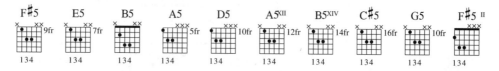

Tune down 1/2 step:
(low to high) E♭-A♭-D♭-G♭-B♭-E♭

Intro
Moderately slow Rock ♩ = 104

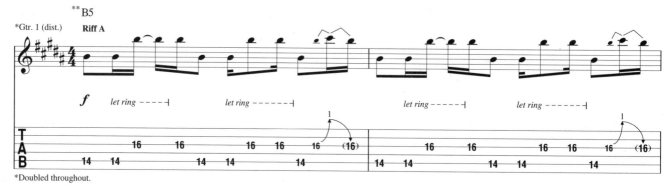

*Doubled throughout.

**Chord symbols reflect overall harmony.

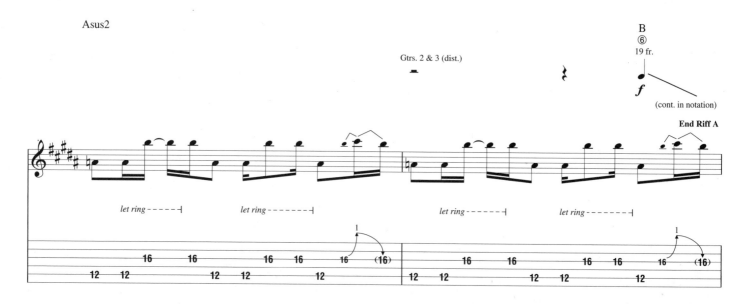

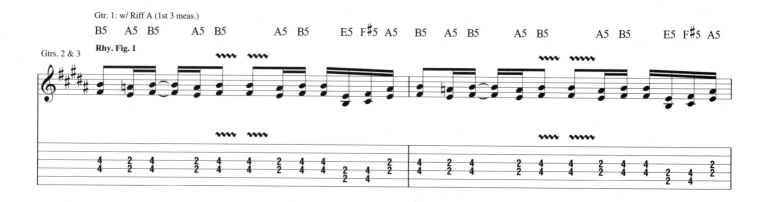

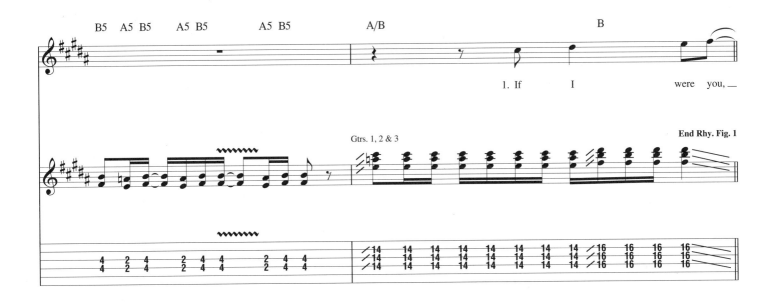

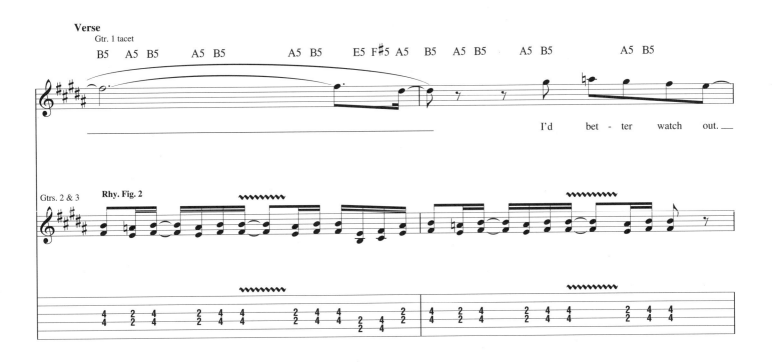

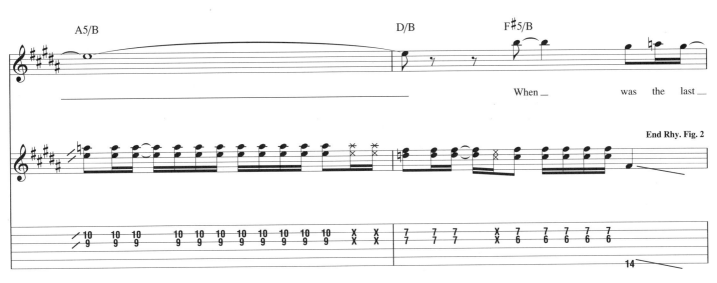

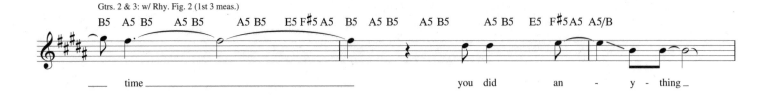

Gtrs. 2 & 3: w/ Rhy. Fig. 2 (1st 3 meas.)

B5 A5 B5   A5 B5   A5 B5   E5 F#5 A5   B5   A5 B5   A5 B5   A5 B5   E5 F#5 A5   A5/B

___ time _____ you did an - y - thing _

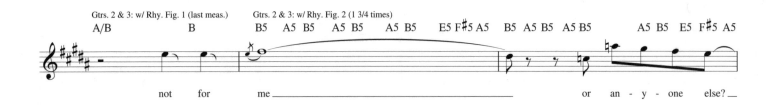

Gtrs. 2 & 3: w/ Rhy. Fig. 1 (last meas.)   Gtrs. 2 & 3: w/ Rhy. Fig. 2 (1 3/4 times)

A/B   B   B5 A5 B5   A5 B5   A5 B5   E5 F#5 A5   B5 A5 B5 A5 B5   A5 B5   E5 F#5 A5

not for me _____ or an - y - one else? _

A5/B   D/B   F#5/B   B5   A5 B5   A5 B5   A5 B5   E5 F#5 A5

_____ Just ___ be - cause? _____

B5   A5 B5   A5 B5   A5 B5   E5 F#5 A5   A5/B   A/B   B

Gtrs. 2 & 3: w/ Rhy. Fig. 1 (last meas.)

___ Just _____ be - cause? _____

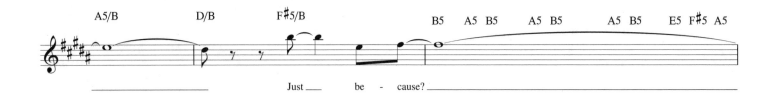

𝄋 Chorus

Gtr. 1: w/ Riff A (1 3/4 times)

B5   D5/B

You, _____   oh, you real - ly should have   known.

Gtrs. 2 & 3

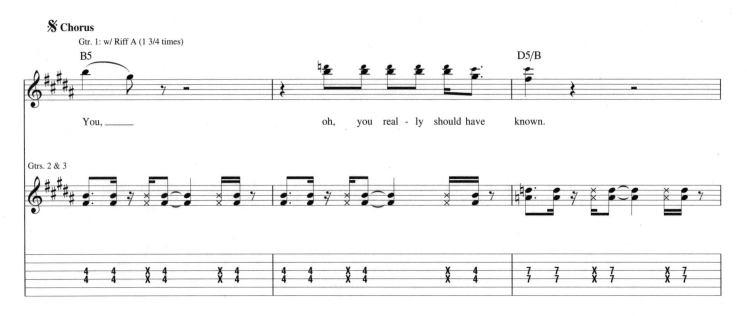

124

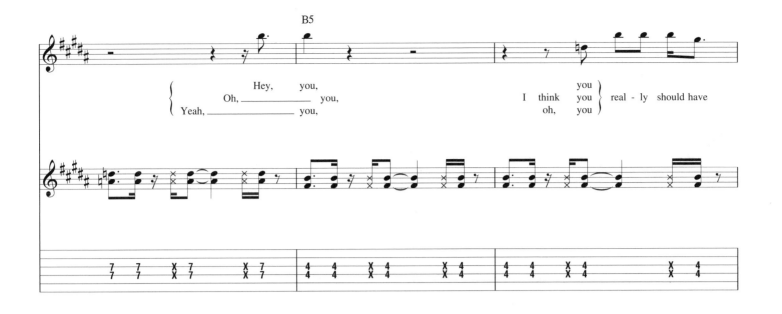

Hey, you,
Oh, ——— you,
Yeah, ——— you,
you
I think you real - ly should have
oh, you

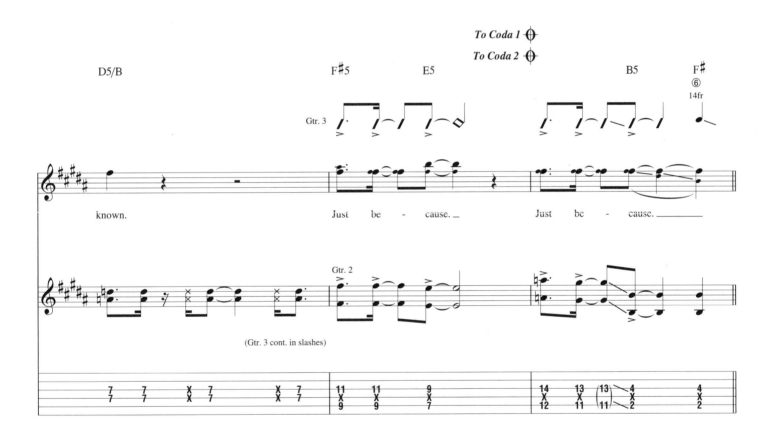

To Coda 1
To Coda 2

D5/B   F#5   E5   B5   F#

Gtr. 3

known.   Just be - cause.   Just be - cause.

Gtr. 2

(Gtr. 3 cont. in slashes)

Interlude

Gtrs. 2 & 3: w/ Rhy. Fig. 1 (1st 3 meas.)

B5 A5 B5   A5 B5   A5 B5   E5 F#5 A5   B5 A5 B5   A5 B5   A5 B5   E5 F#5 A5

Gtr. 4 (dist.)

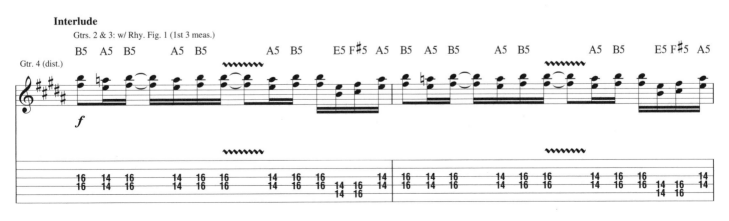

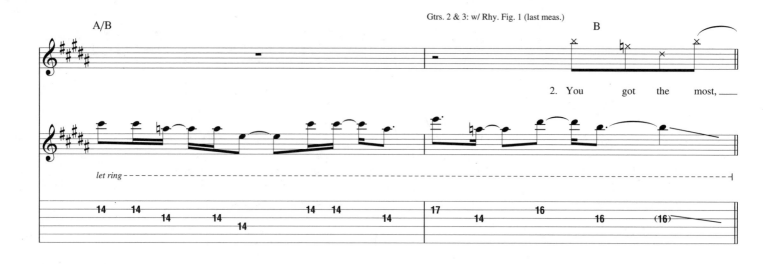

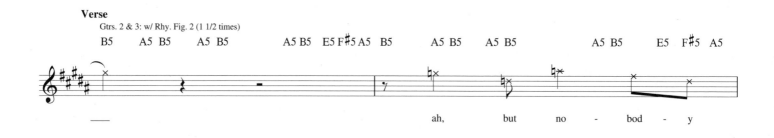

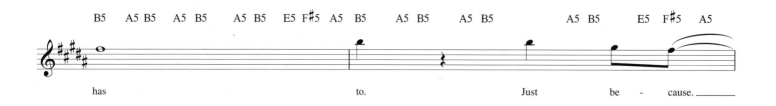

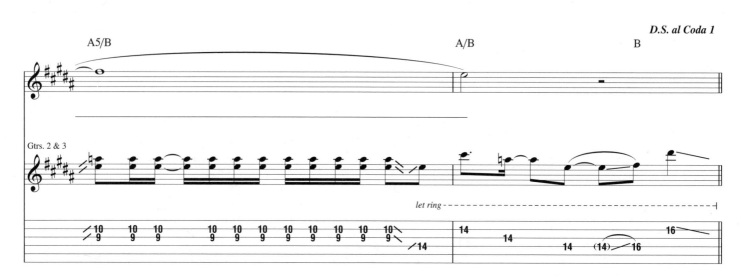

⊕ Coda 1

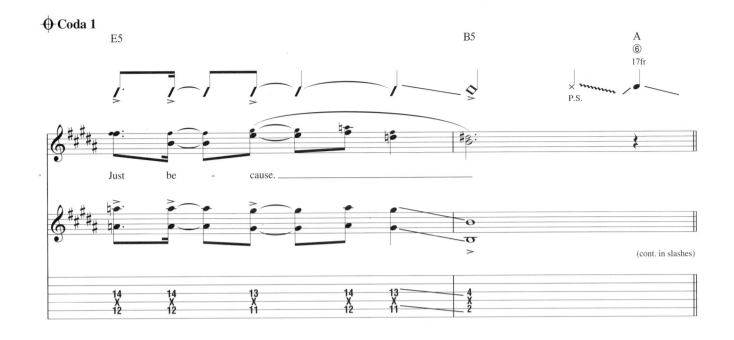

Just be - cause. _____

(cont. in slashes)

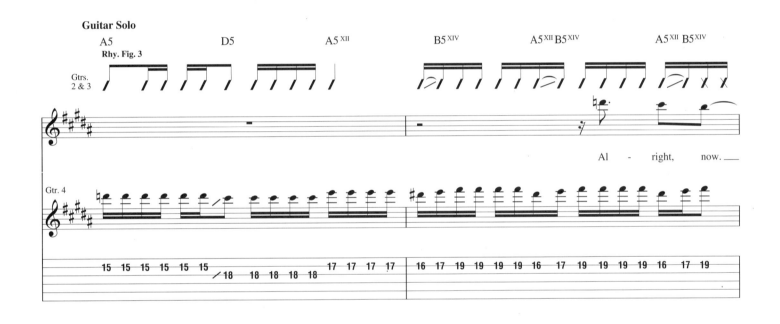

Guitar Solo

Al - right, now. ____

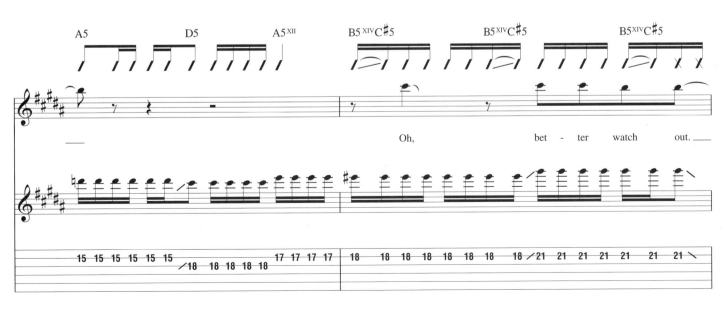

Oh, bet - ter watch out. ____

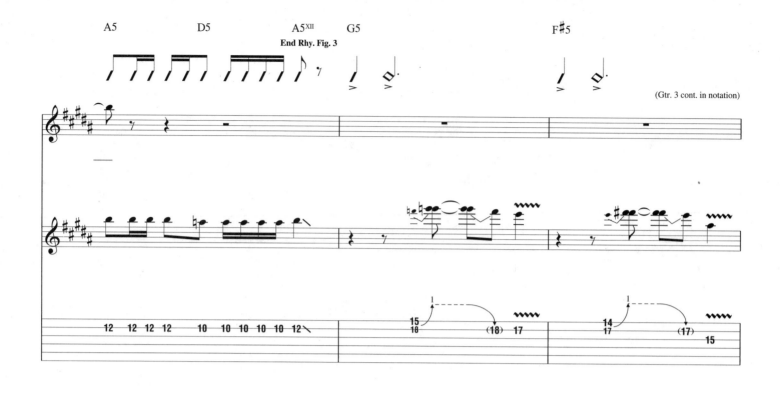

Verse

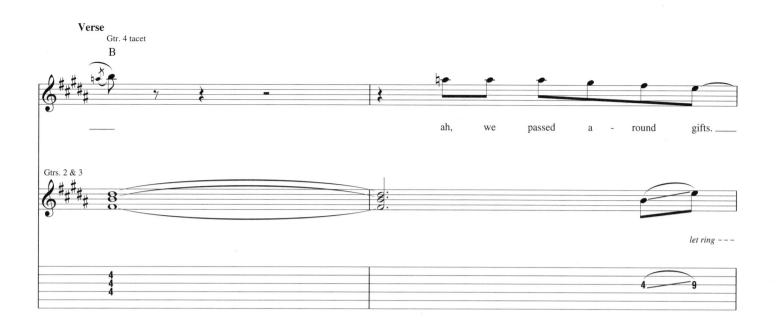

ah, we passed a - round gifts.

That was a long _____ time _____ a -

D.S. al Coda 2

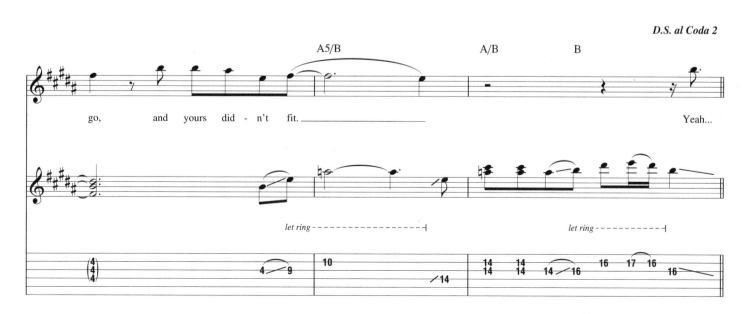

go, and yours did - n't fit. _____ Yeah...

Coda 2

Just be - cause.____ Just be - cause.____

Outro - Guitar Solo

Gtrs. 2 & 3: w/ Rhy. Fig. 3

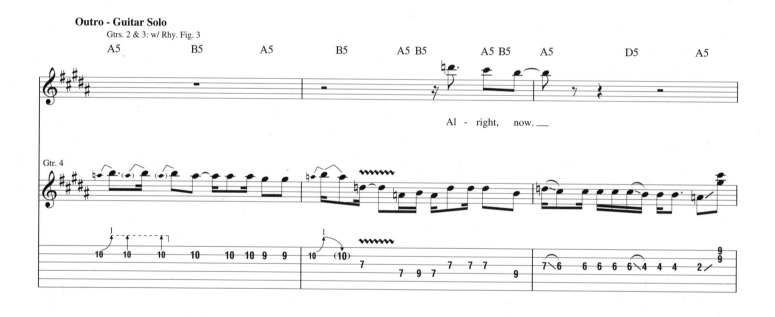

Al - right, now.____

Gtr. 4

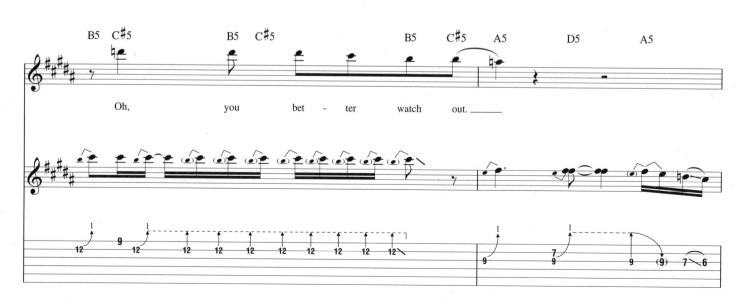

Oh, you bet - ter watch out.____

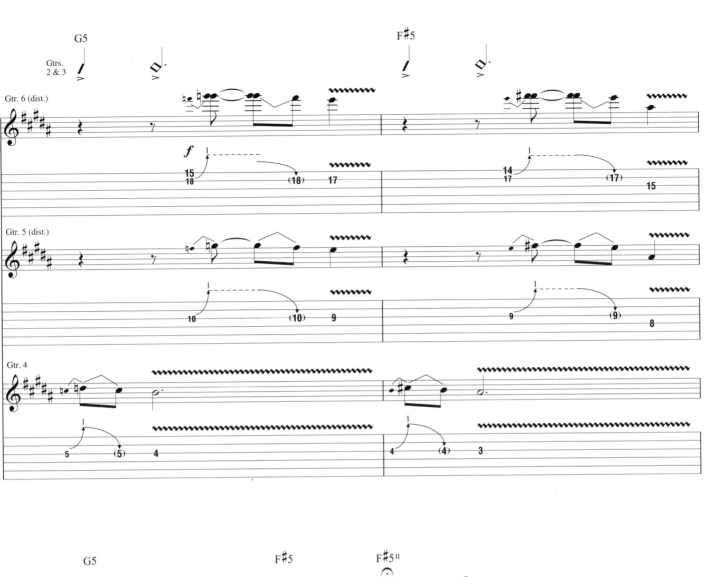

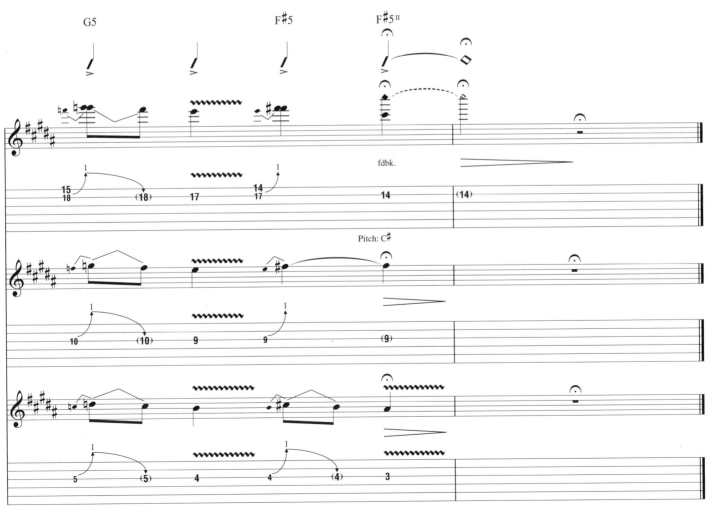

Just Like You

Words and Music by Three Days Grace and Gavin Brown

Kryptonite

Words and Music by Matt Roberts, Brad Arnold and Todd Harrell

Interlude

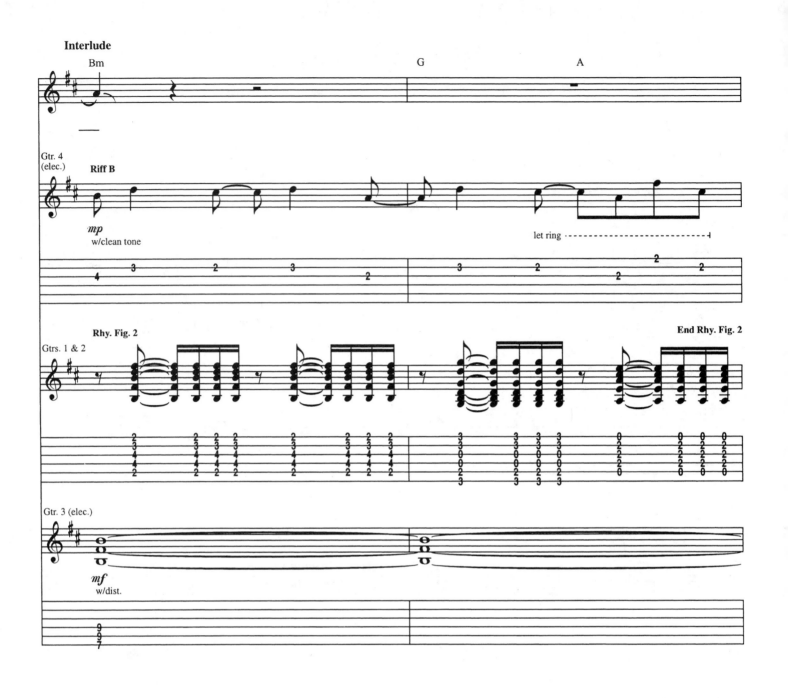

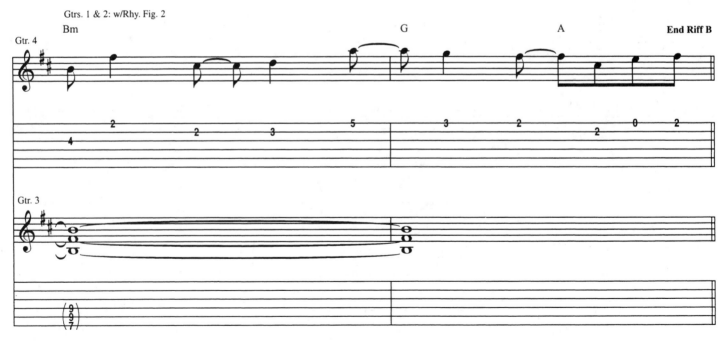

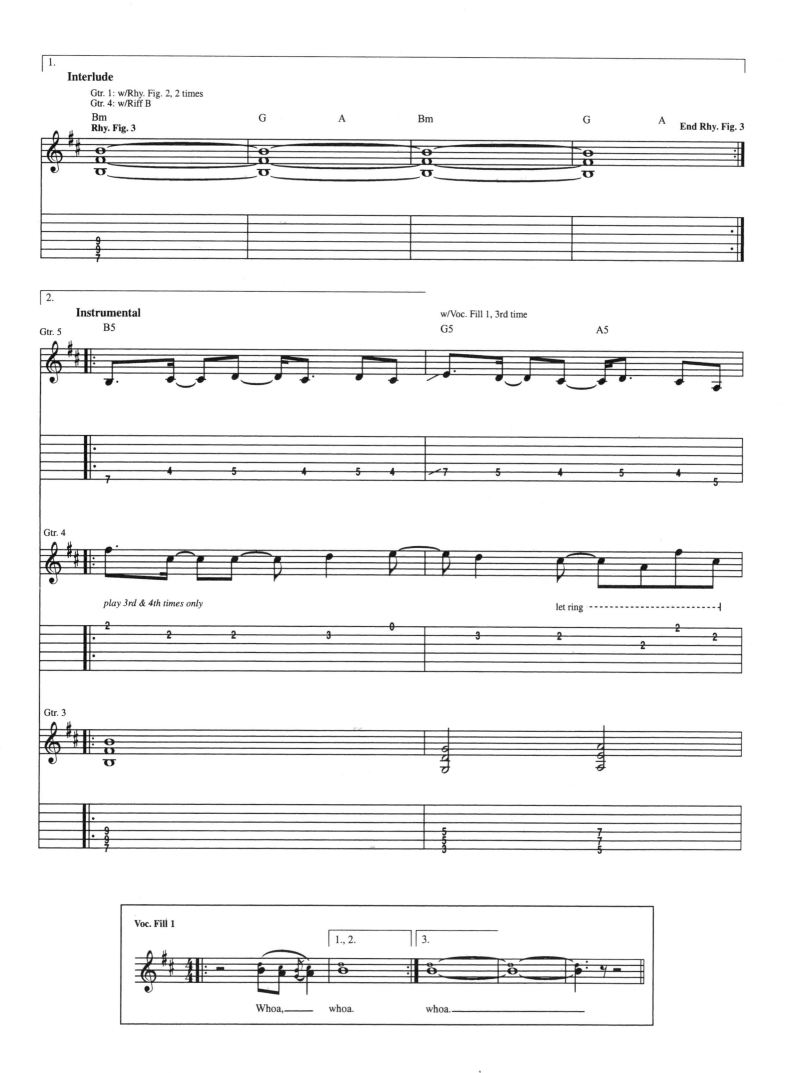

Lifestyles of the Rich and Famous

Words and Music by Benji Madden and Joel Madden

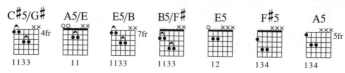

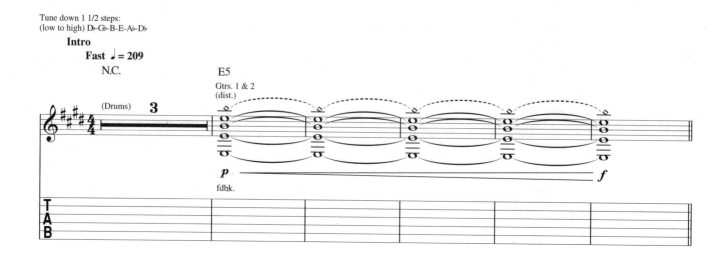

Tune down 1 1/2 steps:
(low to high) Db-Gb-B-E-Ab-Db

Intro
Fast ♩ = 209

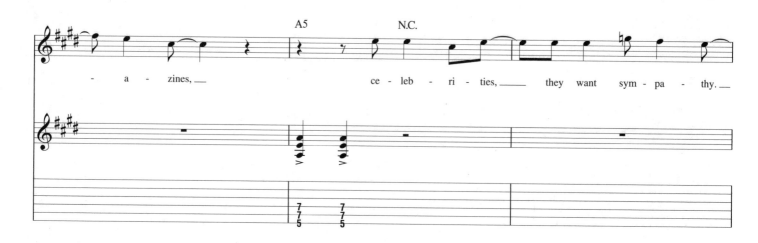

All they do is piss ___ and moan, ___

in - side the Roll - ing Stone, ___ talk - in' a - bout

how hard life can be. ___

Pre-Chorus

I'd like to see ___ them spend ___ a week ___ liv - in' out ___

___ there on ___ the street. ___ I don't think ___ they would ___ sur - vive.

-lem, well, they got man - sions, ____

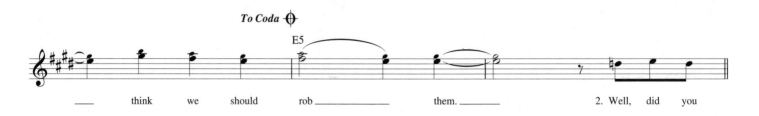

To Coda ⊕

____ think we should rob ____ them. ____ 2. Well, did you

Verse
Gtr. 1: w/ Rhy. Fig. 1 (1 1/2 times)
Gtr. 2: w/ Rhy. Fig. 1 (2 times)

know when you are fa - mous you could kill your wife, ____ and there's no such thing as twen - ty -

five to life ____ as long as you got the cash ____ to pay for Coch -

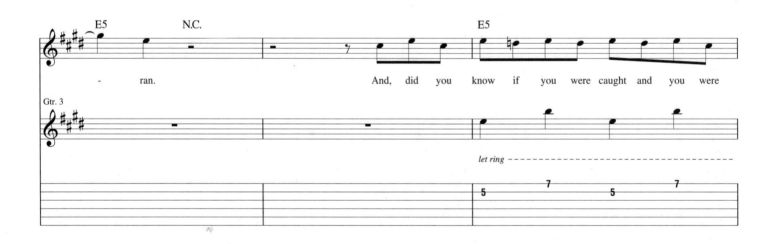

- ran. And, did you know if you were caught and you were

Gtr. 3

let ring -

smok - in' crack, ____ Mc - Don - ald's would - n't e - ven wan - na take you back, ____ you could

let ring -

al - ways just run for may - or of ___ D. C. ___

Pre-Chorus

Gtr. 3: w/ Riff A

I'd like to see ___ them spend ___ a week ___

*Pick eighth-note triplets while sliding down 6th string.

___ liv - in' out ___ there on ___ the street. ___ I don't think ___

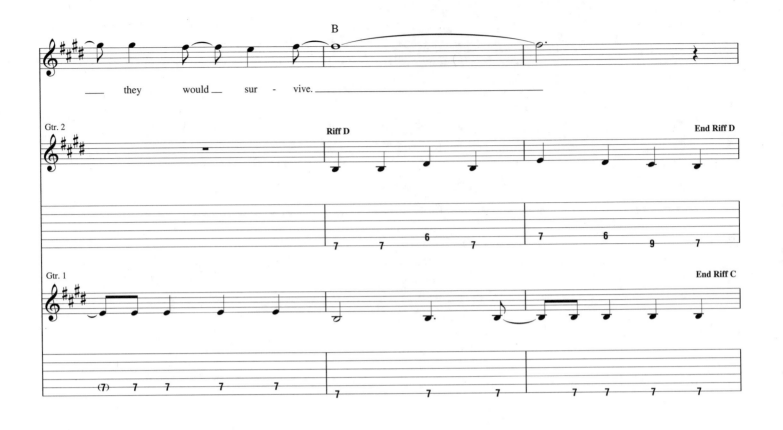

they would sur - vive.

Gtr. 2

Riff D

End Riff D

Gtr. 1

End Riff C

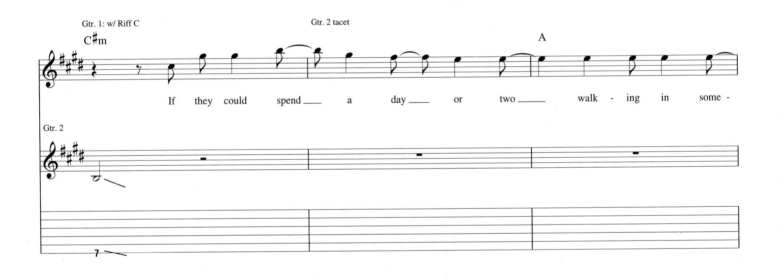

Gtr. 1: w/ Riff C

Gtr. 2 tacet

C#m

A

If they could spend ___ a day ___ or two ___ walk - ing in some -

Gtr. 2

E5

- one else - 's shoes, ___ I think they'd stum -

Gtr. 2: w/ Riff D

B

- ble and ___ they'd fall. ___ They would fall. ___

A

Gtr. 3

let ring

Gtrs. 1 & 2

(cont. in slashes)

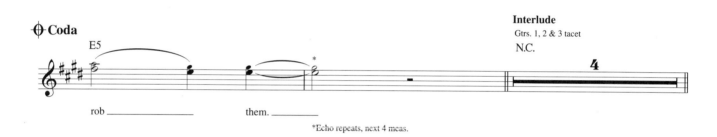

Coda

E5

Interlude

Gtrs. 1, 2 & 3 tacet

N.C.

rob _____ them. _____

*Echo repeats, next 4 meas.

Half-time feel

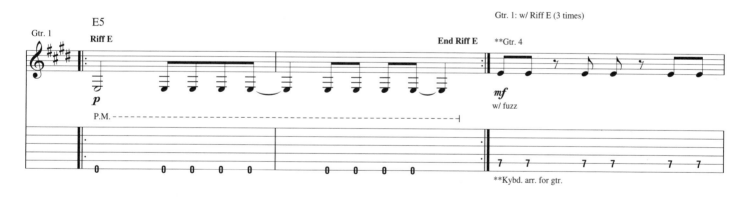

E5

Gtr. 1

Riff E

Gtr. 1: w/ Riff E (3 times)

End Riff E   ****Gtr. 4**

p

mf

w/ fuzz

P.M.

**Kybd. arr. for gtr.

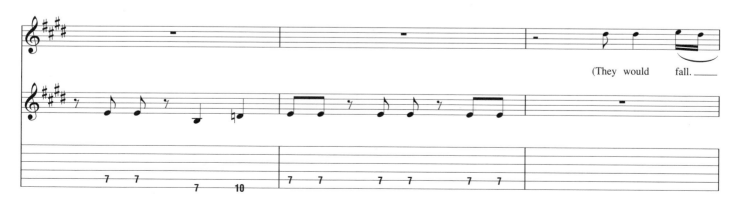

(They would   fall. ____)

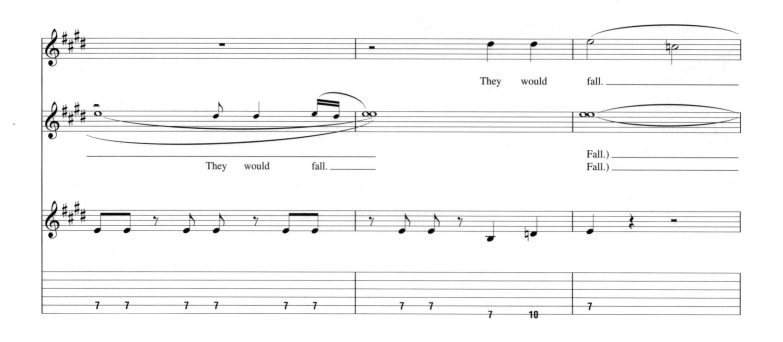

They would fall. _____

They would fall. _____

Fall.) _____

Fall.) _____

Chorus

Gtr. 4 tacet

E5

Life - styles _____ of the rich and the fa -

Gtrs. 1 & 2

Rhy. Fig. 4

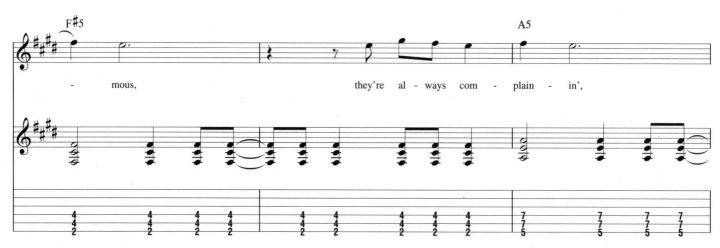

F#5

A5

- mous, they're al - ways com - plain - in',

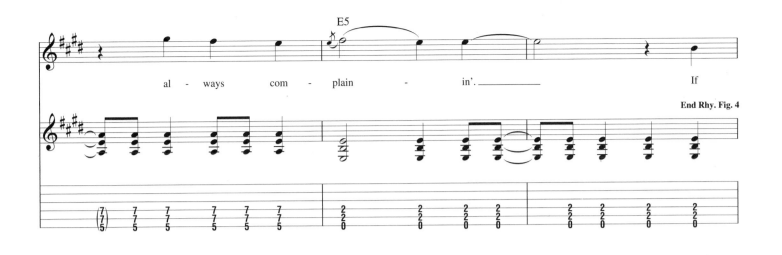

al - ways com - plain - in'.____ If

End Rhy. Fig. 4

Gtrs. 1 & 2: w/ Rhy. Fig. 4

F#5

mon - ey _____ is such a prob - lem, we got so man - y prob -

End half-time feel

Gtrs. 1 & 2: w/ Rhy. Fig. 3

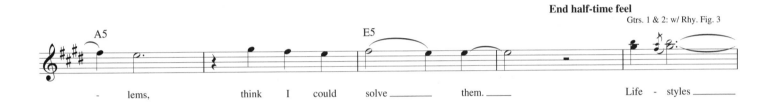

A5   E5

- lems,   think I could solve _____ them. _____   Life - styles _____

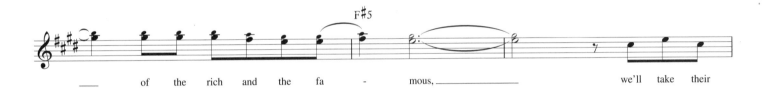

F#5

____ of the rich and the fa - mous, _____ we'll take their

A5   E5

clothes, cash, cars, and homes ____ just stop com - plain - in'. _____

Outro

A5

____   Life - styles _____ of the

Rhy. Fig. 5

Gtrs. 1 & 2

rich   and   fa - mous.   Life - styles _____

_____   of   the   rich   and   fa -   mous.

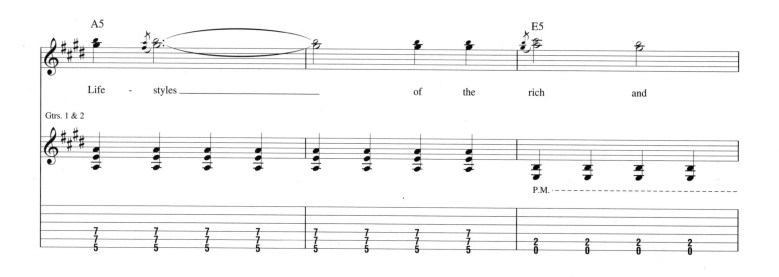

Life - styles _____   of   the   rich   and

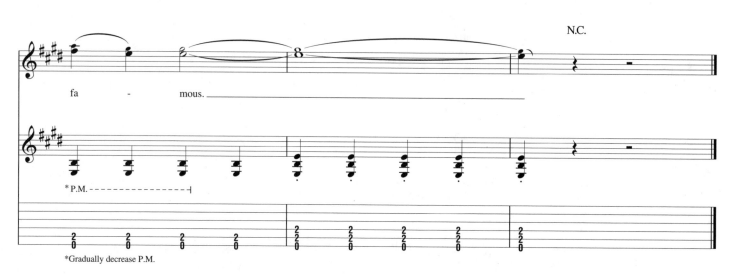

fa -   mous. _____

*Gradually decrease P.M.

Like a Stone

Lyrics by Chris Cornell
Music written and arranged by Audioslave

*Gtrs. 1, 2, 4 & 5: Capo III

Intro

Moderately ♩ = 112

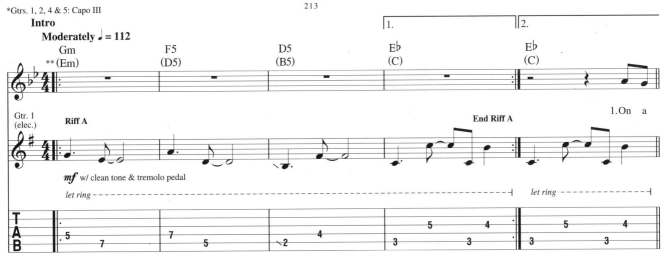

*This song was recorded using guitars with ultra light strings, and tuned up 1 1/2 steps. To avoid warped necks,
broken strings and personal injury, remain in standard tuning and capo at the 3rd fret.

**Symbols in parentheses represent chord names relative to capoed guitars. Symbols above reflect
actual sounding chords, Capoed fret is "0" in tab. Chord symbols reflect implied harmony.

Verse

Gtr. 1: w/ Riff A (4 times)

cob - web af - ter - noon _____ in a _____ room full _____ of emp - ti - ness _____ by a
death - bed I will pray _____ to the gods and the an - gels like a

free - way, I con - fess, _____ I was _____ lost in _____ the pag - es _____
pa - gan to an - y - one _____ who will _____ take me _____ to heav - en,

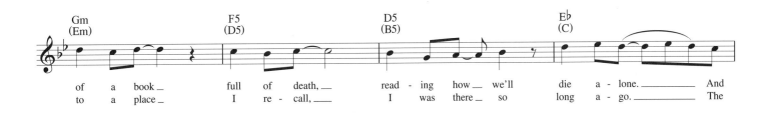

of a book _____ full of death, _____ read - ing how we'll die a - lone. _____ And
to a place _____ I re - call, _____ I was there so long a - go. _____ The

if we're good _____ we'll lay to rest _____ an - y - where we want to go. _____
sky was bruised, _____ the wine was bled, _____ and there you led _____ me on. _____

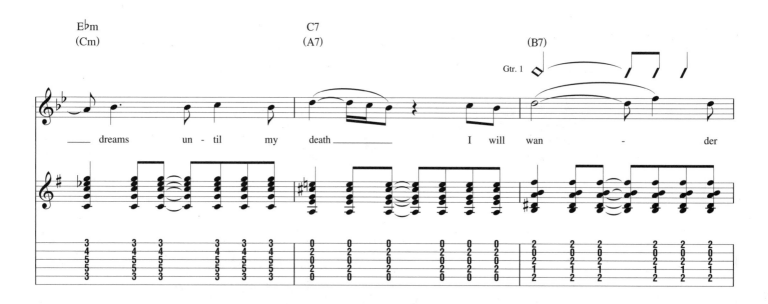

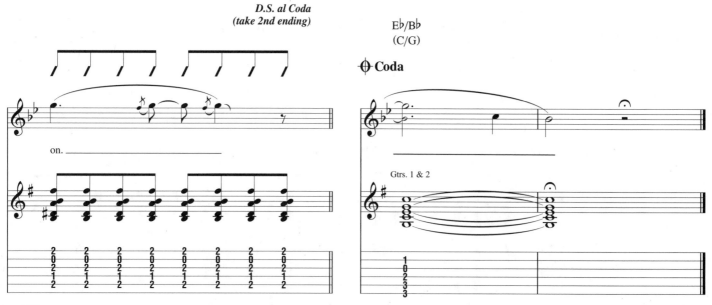

Maps

Words and Music by Karen Orzolek, Nick Zinner and Brian Chase

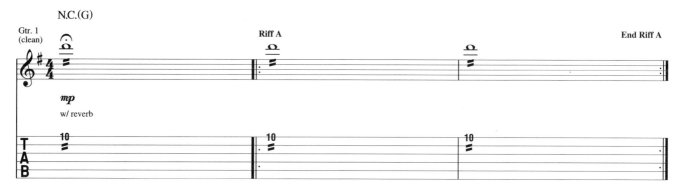

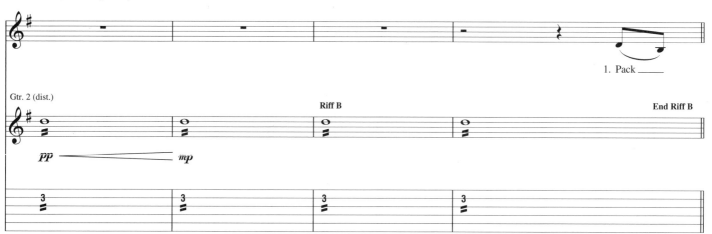

*Chord symbols reflect implied harmmony.

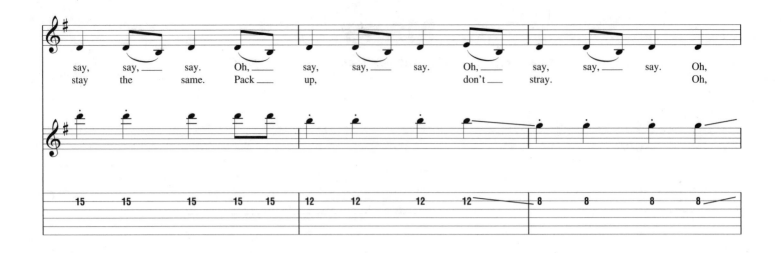

say, say, ___ say. Oh, ___ say, say, ___ say. Oh, ___ say, say, ___ say. Oh,
stay the same. Pack ___ up, don't ___ stray. Oh,

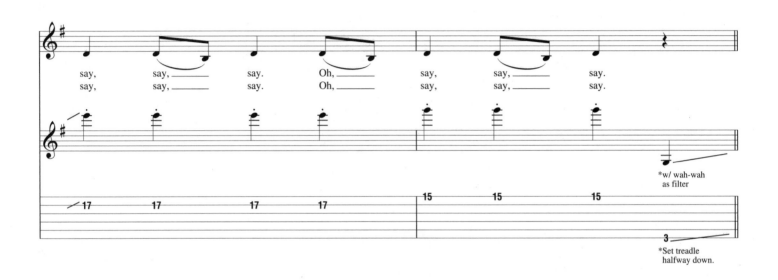

say, say, ___ say. Oh, ___ say, say, ___ say.
say, say, ___ say. Oh, ___ say, say, ___ say.

*w/ wah-wah
as filter

*Set treadle
halfway down.

𝄋 Chorus

1st time, Gtr. 1: w/ Riff A (4 times)
1st time, Gtr. 2: w/ Riff B (4 times)
2nd & 3rd times, Gtr. 1: w/ Riff A (8 times)
2nd & 3rd times, Gtr. 2: w/ Riff B (8 times)
3rd time, Gtr. 6 tacet

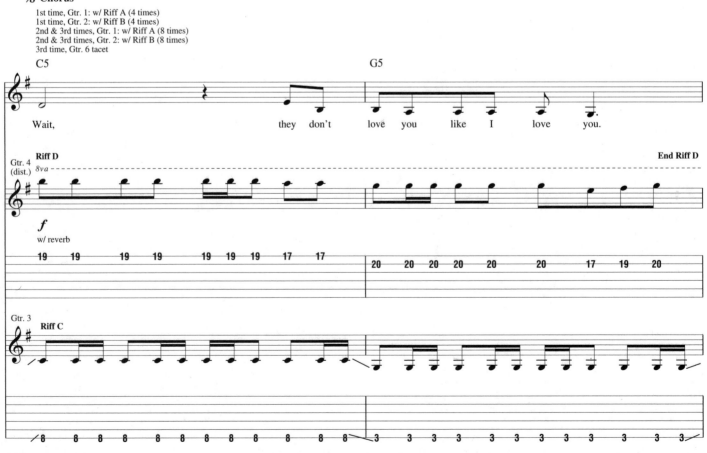

C5   G5

Wait,   they don't love you like I love you.

Gtr. 4 (dist.) **Riff D** *8va* - **End Riff D**

f
w/ reverb

Gtr. 3 **Riff C**

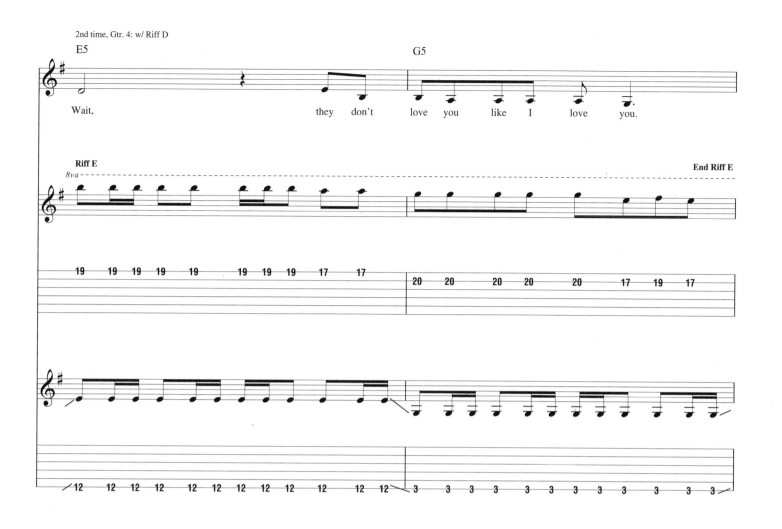

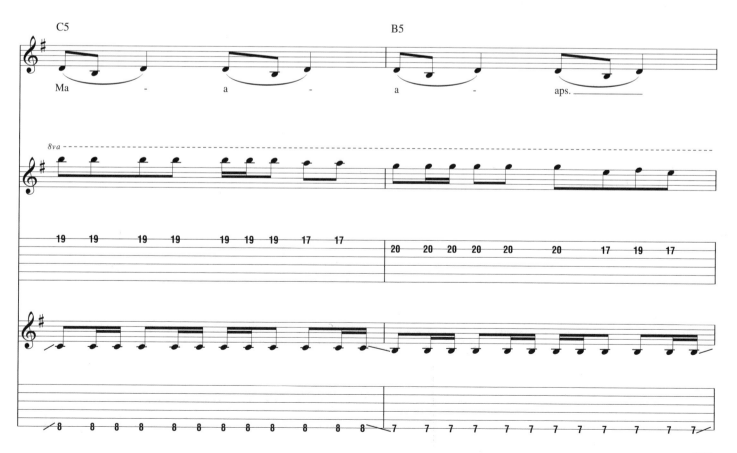

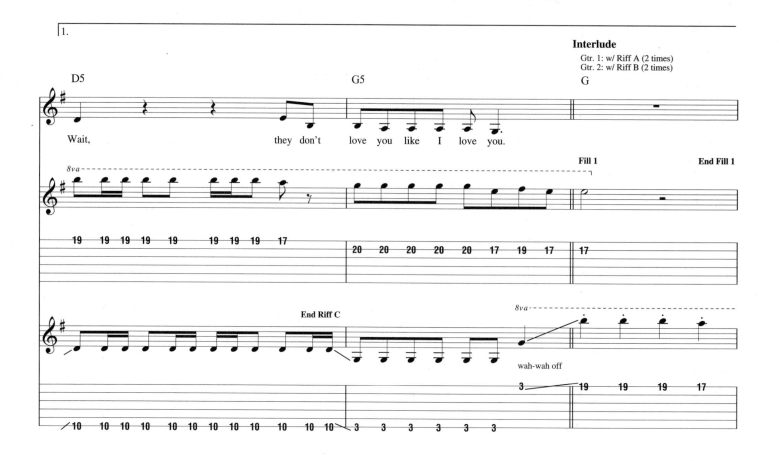

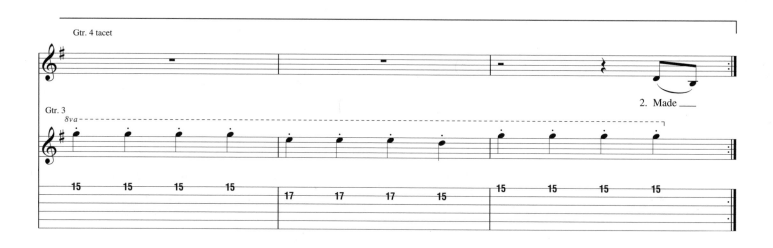

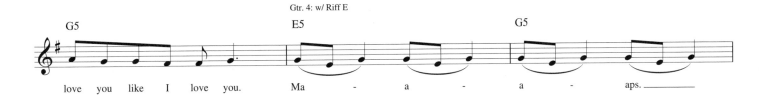

love you like I love you. Ma - a - a - aps. _____

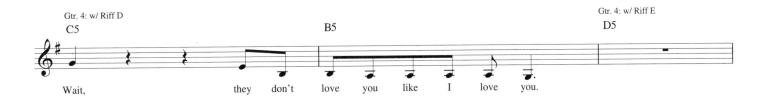

Wait, they don't love you like I love you.

Interlude
Gtr. 1: w/ Riff A (4 times)
Gtr. 2: w/ Riff B (4 times)
Gtr. 4: w/ Fill 1

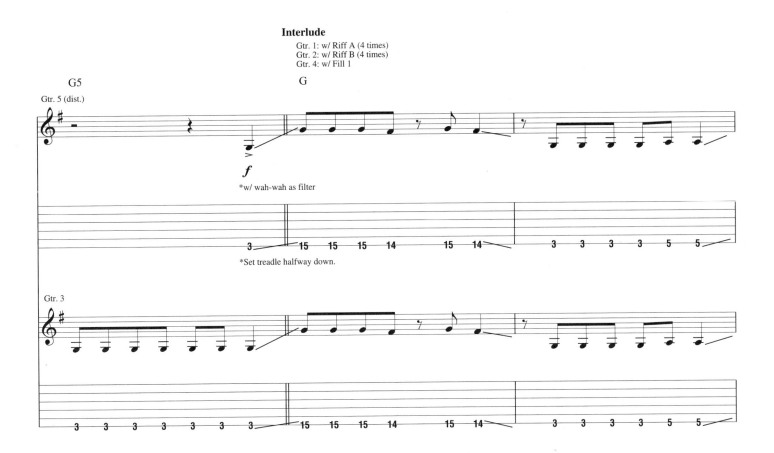

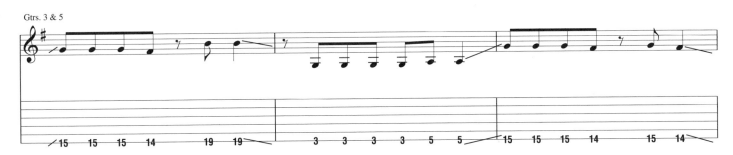

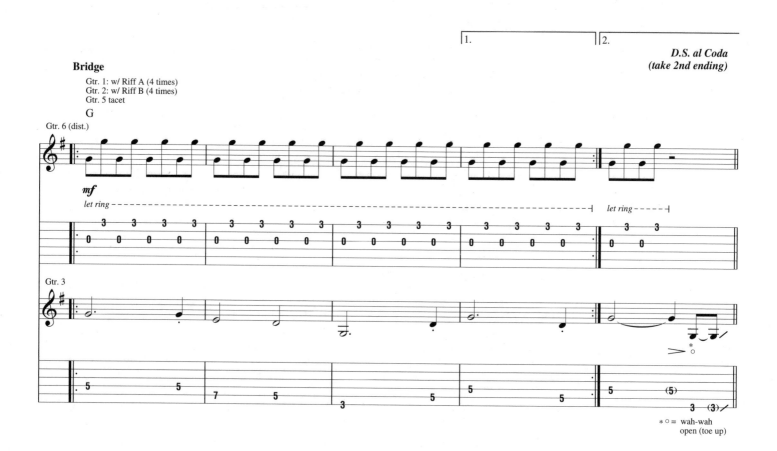

*○ = wah-wah
open (toe up)

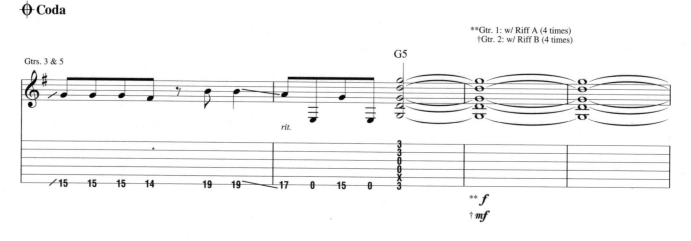

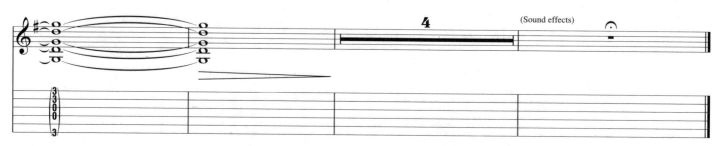

So Cold

Words and Music by Benjamin Burnley, Jeremy Hummel, Aaron C. Fincke and Mark J. Klepaski

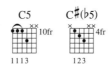

Drop D tuning, down 1 step:
(low to high) C-G-C-F-A-D

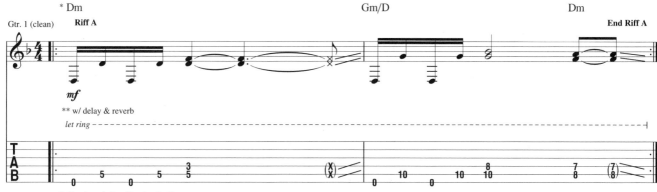

* Chord symbols reflect implied harmony.
** Delay set for eigth-note regeneration w/ 2 repeats.

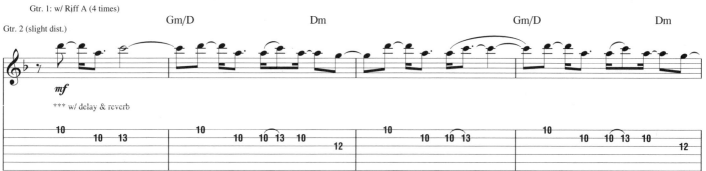

***Delay set for eighth-note regeneration w/ 2 repeats.

·*Doubled by bass.

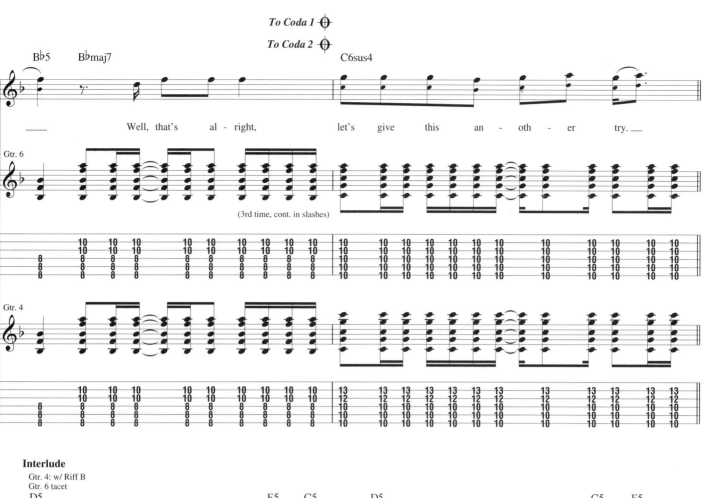

Well, that's al - right, let's give this an - oth - er try. ___

Interlude

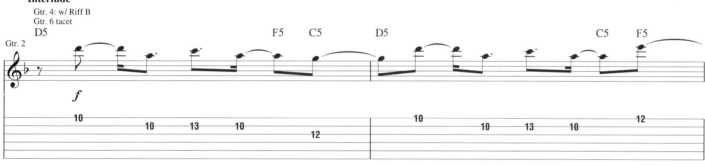

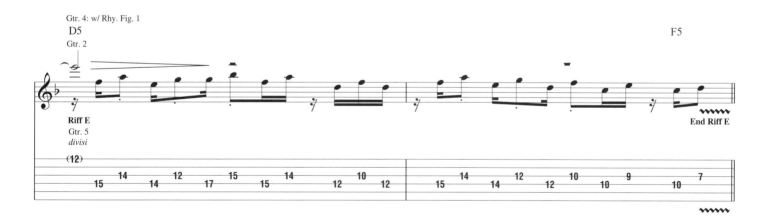

Verse

2. If you find ___ your fam - i - ly, don't ___ you ___ cry.

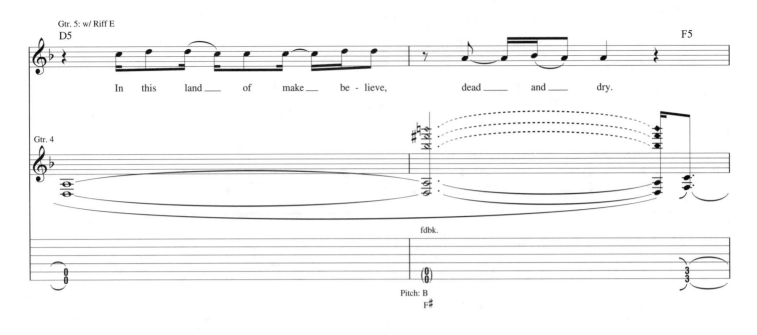

Gtr. 5: w/ Riff E

In this land of make be-lieve, dead and dry.

Gtr. 4

fdbk.

Pitch: B
F#

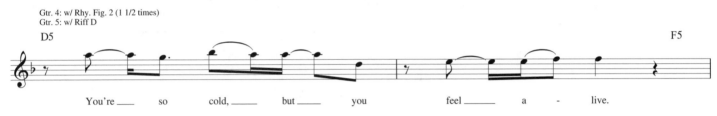

Gtr. 4: w/ Rhy. Fig. 2 (1 1/2 times)
Gtr. 5: w/ Riff D

You're so cold, but you feel a - live.

D.S. al Coda 1

Gtrs. 4 & 6: w/ Rhy. Fills 1 & 1A

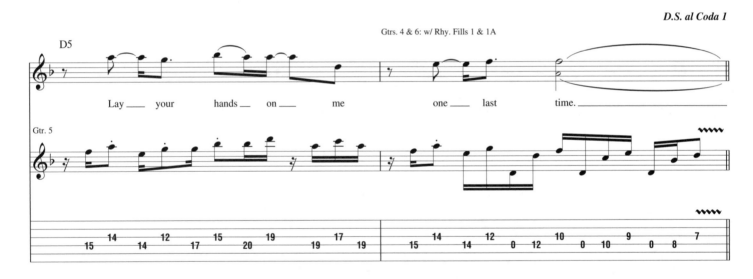

Lay your hands on me one last time.

Gtr. 5

⊕ **Coda 1**

Interlude

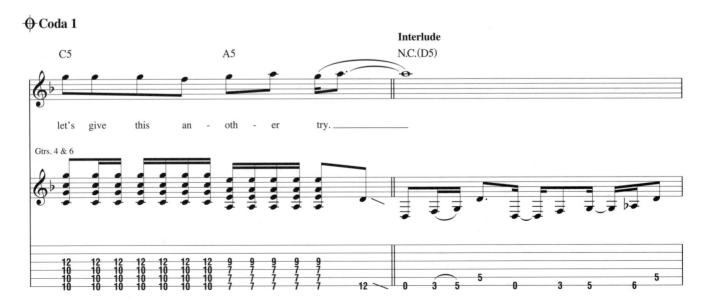

let's give this an-oth-er try.

Gtrs. 4 & 6

Somebody Told Me

Words and Music by Brandon Flowers, Dave Keuning, Mark Stoermer and Ronnie Vannucci

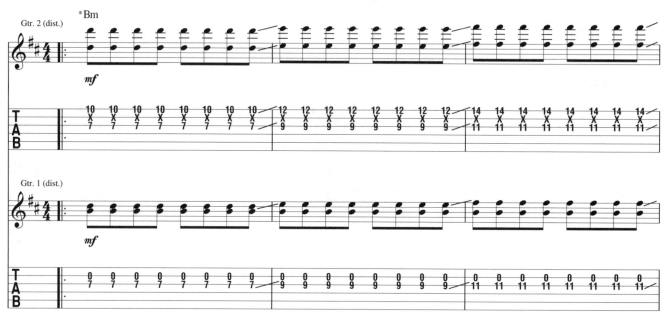

*Chord symbols reflect overall harmony.

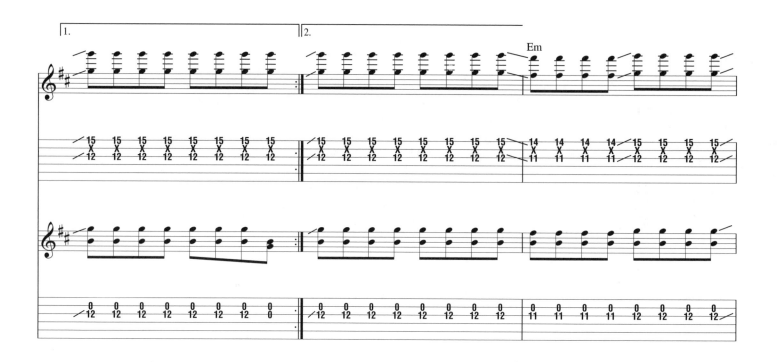

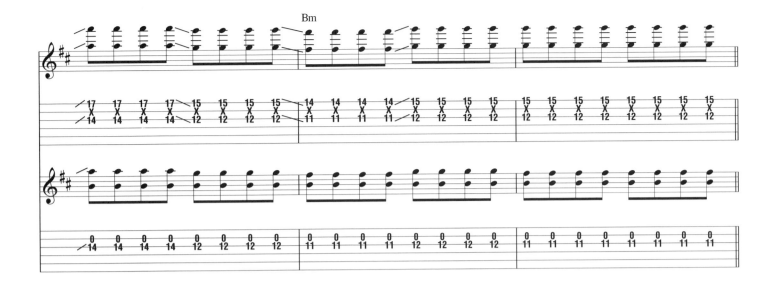

Verse

Gtr. 2 tacet

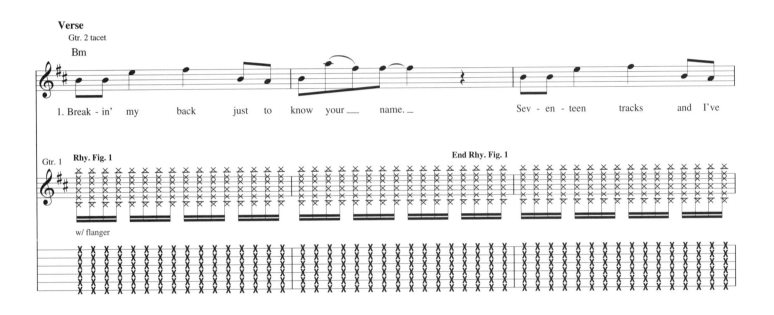

1. Break - in' my back just to know your ___ name. ___ Sev - en - teen tracks and I've

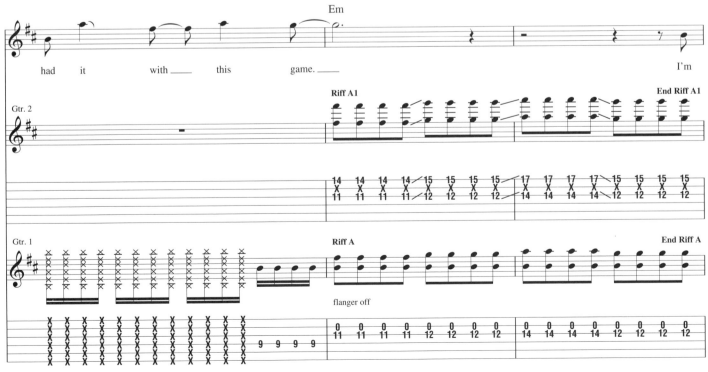

had it with ___ this game. ___ I'm

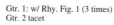

Gtr. 1: w/ Rhy. Fig. 1 (3 times)
Gtr. 2 tacet

Bm

break-in' my back just to know your ___ name, ___ but heav-en ain't close ___ in a place like ___ this. ___

Gtrs. 1 & 2: w/ Riffs A & A1

Em

An-y-thing goes, but don't ___ blink, ___ you ___ might miss. _____ 'Cause

Gtr. 1: w/ Rhy. Fig. 1 (2 times)

Bm

heav-en ain't close ___ in a place like ___ this. I said, uh, heav-en ain't close ___ in a place like this. ___

Pre-Chorus

G5/D   D5   Bsus4   Bm

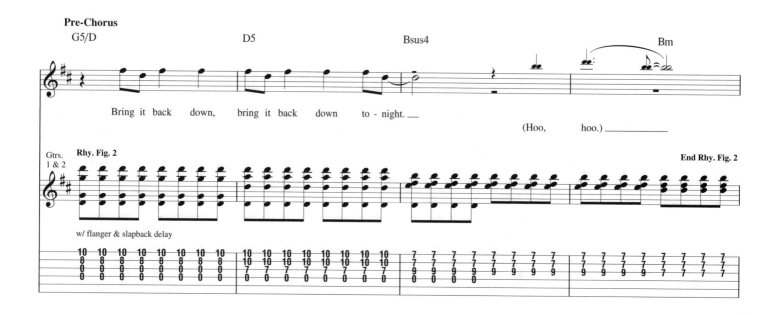

Bring it back down, bring it back down to - night. ___

(Hoo,   hoo.) _____

Gtrs. 1 & 2   **Rhy. Fig. 2**   **End Rhy. Fig. 2**

w/ flanger & slapback delay

G5/D   D5   N.C.

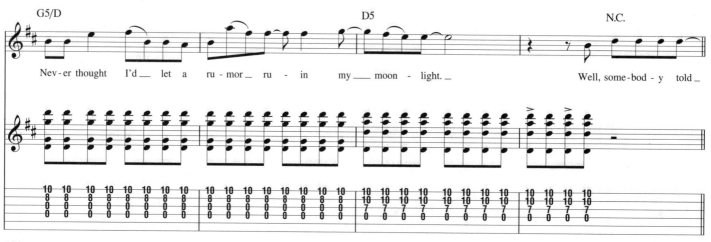

Nev-er thought I'd ___ let a ru-mor ru-in my ___ moon - light. ___

Well, some-bod-y told ___

Chorus

___ me you had a boy - friend who looked like a girl - friend that I had in Feb -

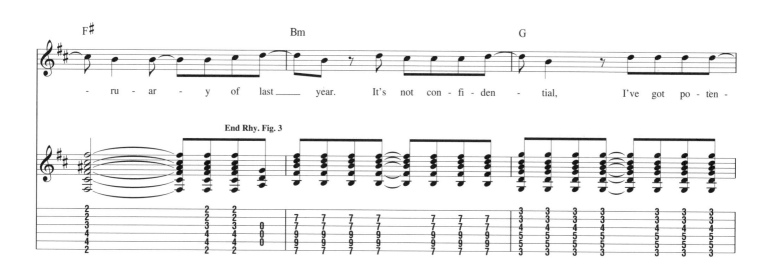

-ru-ar-y of last ___ year. It's not con-fi-den-tial, I've got po-ten-

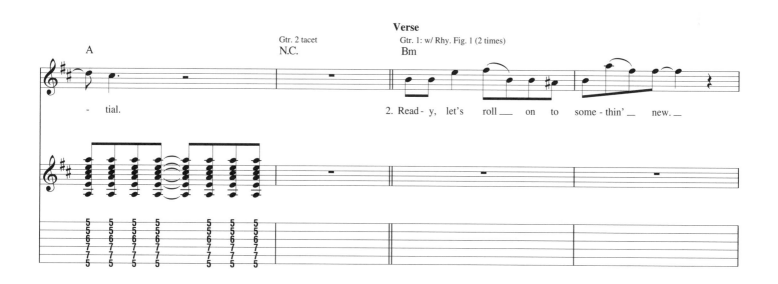

-tial.   2. Read - y, let's roll ___ on to some-thin' ___ new. ___

Tak - in' its toll ___ and I'm leav - in' ___ with - out you. ___   'Cause

Gtr. 1: w/ Rhy. Fig. 1 (2 times)

heav-en ain't close _ in a place like _ this. I said, uh, heav-en ain't close _ in a place like this. _

Pre-Chorus

Gtrs. 1 & 2: w/ Rhy. Fig. 2

Bring it back down, bring it back down to-night. _____ (Hoo, hoo.) _____

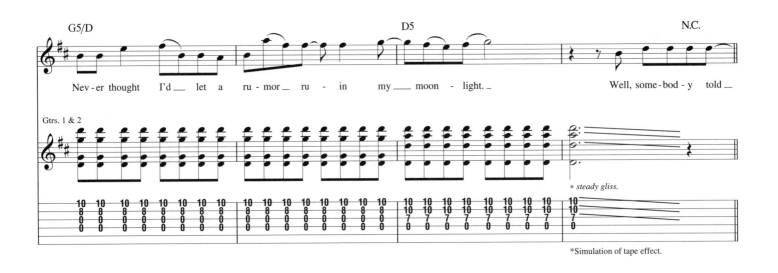

Nev-er thought I'd _ let a ru-mor _ ru-in my _ moon-light. _ Well, some-bod-y told _

*steady gliss.

*Simulation of tape effect.

Chorus

Gtrs. 1 & 2: w/ Rhy. Fig. 3 (1 1/2 times)

_____ me you had a boy-friend who looked like a girl-friend that I had in Feb-ru-ar-y of last

_____ year. It's not con-fi-den - tial, I've got po-ten - tial, a rush-in', a rush-in' a-round.

Chorus

— me you had a boy - friend who looked like a girl - friend that I had in Feb -

- ru - ar - y of last ___ year. It's not con - fi - den - tial, I've got po - ten -

1.
Gtrs. 1 & 2: w/ Rhy. Fig. 4

2.
Gtrs. 1 & 2: w/ Rhy. Fig. 4

- tial, a rush - in', a rush - in' a - round. Now some - bod - y told ___ - tial, a rush - in', a rush -

- in' a - round. Some - bod - y told ___ me you had a boy - friend who looked like a girl -

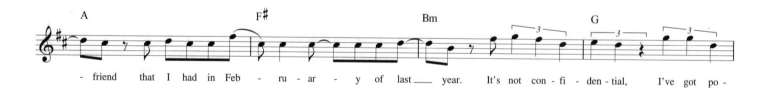

- friend that I had in Feb - ru - ar - y of last ___ year. It's not con - fi - den - tial, I've got po -

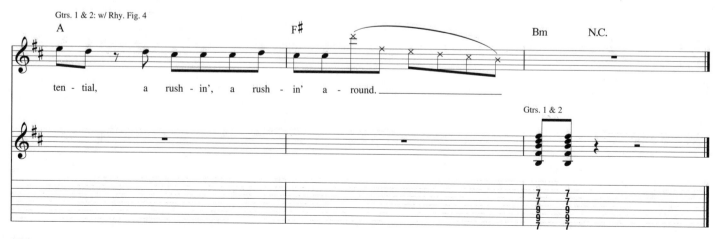

ten - tial, a rush - in', a rush - in' a - round. ___

The Space Between

Words and Music by David J. Matthews and Glen Ballard

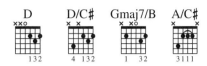

All gtrs.: Tune down 2 1/2 steps:
(low to high) B–E–A–D–F#–B

Verse

Moderately slow ♩ = 88

1. You can-not quit __ me so quick - ly. _____
2. These fick - le, fud - dled words con - fuse me,

* Gtr. 1
(clean)

mf

* Baritone gtr. arr. for standard gtr.; doubled throughout (music sounds a 4th lower than indicated).

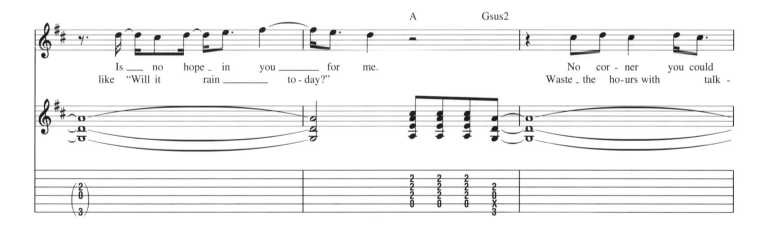

Is __ no hope __ in you _____ for me.
like "Will it rain _____ to - day?"

No cor - ner you could
Waste _ the ho - urs with talk -

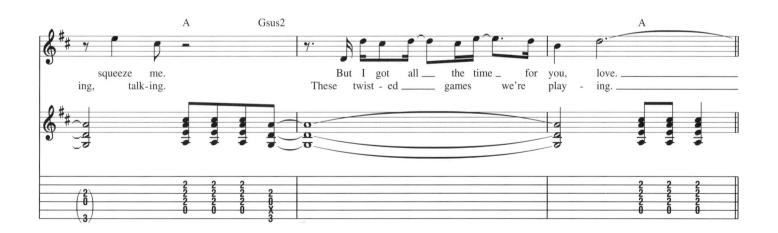

squeeze me.
ing, talk-ing.

But I got all ___ the time _ for you, love. _____
These twist - ed _____ games we're play - ing. _____

Bridge

Look at us spin-ning out in the mad - ness of a roll - er coast - er. __ You know you went off like the dev - il in a

Fill 1

End Fill 1

* Gtr. 4

Gtr. 1

* Sax arr. for gtr.

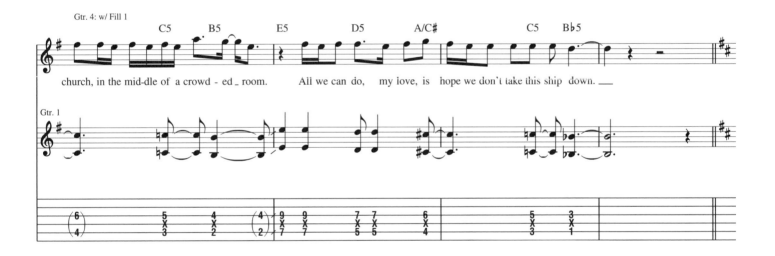

Gtr. 4: w/ Fill 1

church, in the mid-dle of a crowd - ed __ room. All we can do, my love, is hope we don't take this ship down. __

Gtr. 1

Chorus

Gtr. 2: w/ Rhy. Fig. 1 (6 times)

Gtr. 3: w/ Riff A (6 times)

Gtr. 1 & band tacet

The space be - tween _____ where you _____ smile _____ and hide, _____ that's where you'll find _

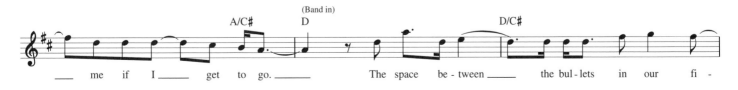

___ me if I ___ get to go. ___ The space be - tween _____ the bul - lets in our fi -

183

Take a Look Around
(Theme From "M:I-2")
from the Paramount Motion Picture M:I-2

Words and Music by Fred Durst and Lalo Schifrin

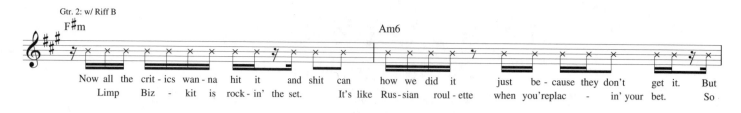

Gtr. 2: w/ Riff B

F#m ... Am6

Now all the crit-ics wan-na hit it and shit can how we did it just be-cause they don't get it. But
Limp Biz-kit is rock-in' the set. It's like Rus-sian roul-ette when you're replac - in' your bet. So

D6 ... D/E

I'll stay fit-ted new er-a com-mit-ed. Now this red cap gets a rap from his crit-ics.
don't be up-set when you're broke and you're done, 'cause I'm a be the one 'til I jet.

1. **Gtr. 1: w/ Riff A**

N.C.(F#m) ... (A)

But do we al-ways got-ta cry? Do we al-ways got-ta live in-side a lie?
(Al - ways got - ta cry?) Live in-side a lie?)

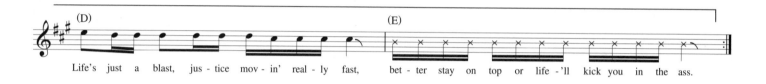

(D) ... (E)

Life's just a blast, jus-tice mov-in' real-ly fast, bet-ter stay on top or life-'ll kick you in the ass.

2. **% Chorus**

N.C.

I know why you wan-na hate me. I know why you wan-na hate me.

Gtr. 3
(dist.)

Riff C ... **End Riff C**

Gtr. 3: w/ Riff C (3 times)

I know why you wan-na hate me. 'Cause hate is all the world has e-ven seen late-ly.

Gtr. 4 (dist.): w/ Riff C (2 times)

I know why you wan-na hate me. I know why you wan-na hate me.

Now I know why you wan-na hate me. 'Cause hate is all the world's e - ven seen late - ly.

F#5   A5 B5   F#5   E#5   F#5   A5 B5

And now you wan-na hate me 'cause

Gtrs. 3 & 4

F#5   E#5   F#5   A5 B5   F#5   E#5

hate is all the world has e - ven seen late - ly.

Rhy. Fig. 1   End Rhy. Fig. 1

P.M. P.M. P.M. P.M.   P.M. P.M. P.M. P.M.

To Coda ⊕

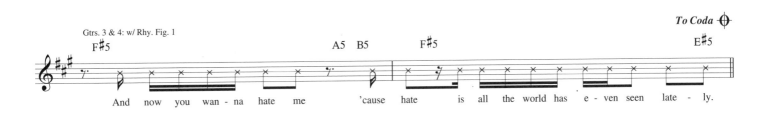

Gtrs. 3 & 4: w/ Rhy. Fig. 1

F#5   A5 B5   F#5   E#5

And now you wan-na hate me 'cause hate is all the world has e - ven seen late - ly.

Interlude

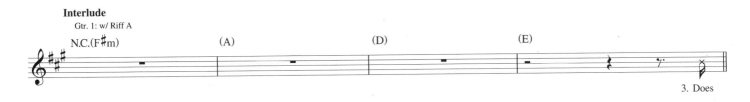

Gtr. 1: w/ Riff A

N.C.(F#m)   (A)   (D)   (E)

3. Does

Verse

Gtr. 2: w/ Riff B (4 times)

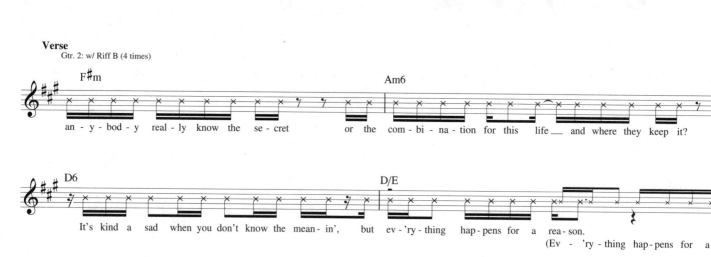

an-y-bod-y real-ly know the se-cret or the com-bi-na-tion for this life __ and where they keep it?

It's kind a sad when you don't know the mean-in', but ev-'ry-thing hap-pens for a rea-son.
(Ev-'ry-thing hap-pens for a

I don't e-ven know what I should say 'cause I'm an id-i-ot, a los-er, mic-ro-phone a-bus-er.
rea-son.)

I an-a-lize ev-'ry sec-ond I ex-ist, beat-in' up my mind ev-'ry sec-ond with my fists.

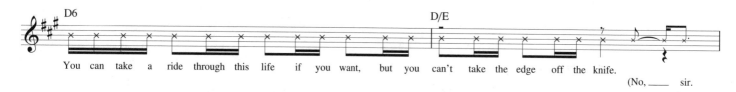

And ev-'ry-bod-y wan-na run, ev-'ry-bod-y wan-na hide from the gun.
(Wan-na run, hide from the gun.)

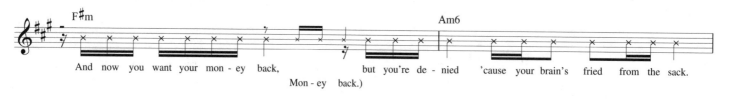

You can take a ride through this life if you want, but you can't take the edge off the knife.
(No, __ sir.

And now you want your mon-ey back, but you're de-nied 'cause your brain's fried from the sack.
Mon-ey back.)

D.S. al Coda

And there ain't noth-in' I can __ do 'cause life is a les-son. You'll learn it when you're through.

⊕ Coda

Gtrs. 3 & 4

188

This Love

Words and Music by Adam Levine and Jesse Carmichael

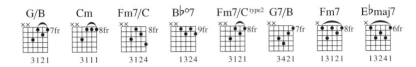

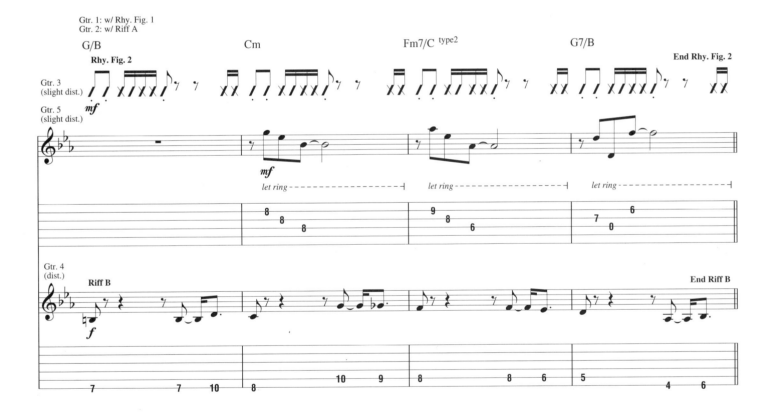

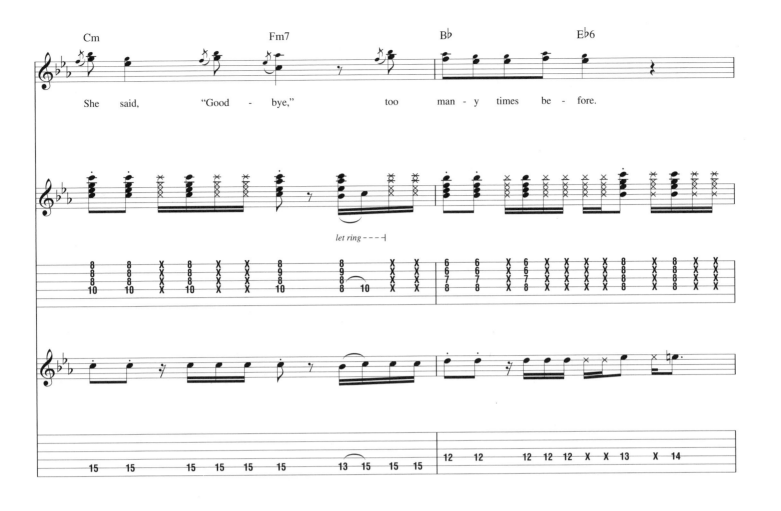

She said, "Good - bye," too man - y times be - fore.

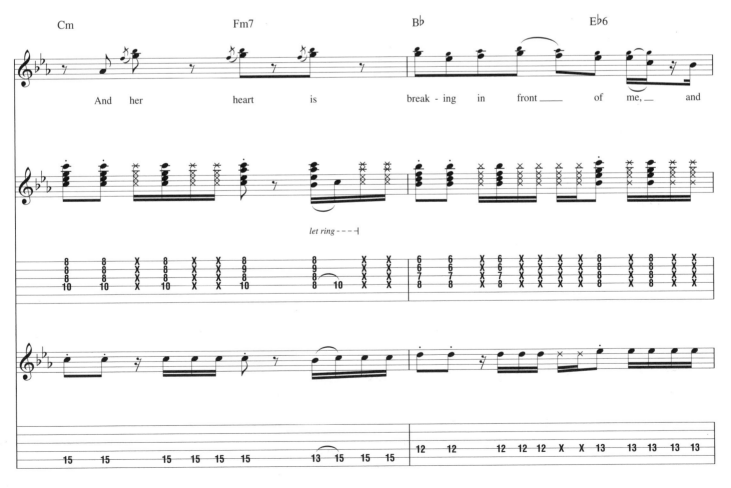

And her heart is break - ing in front ___ of me, ___ and

194

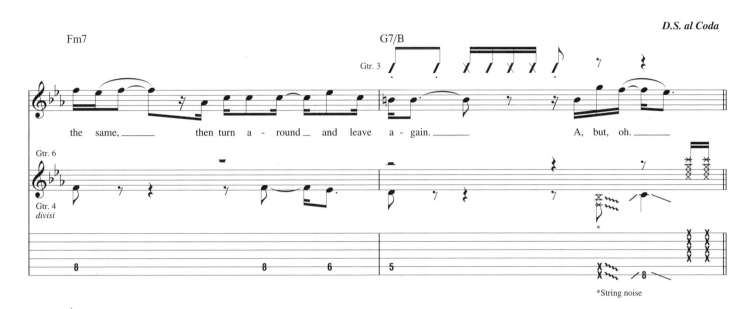

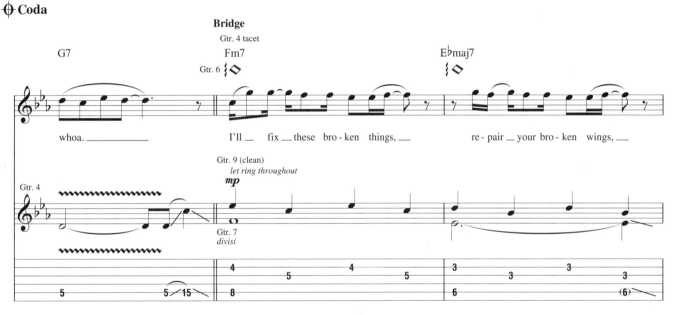

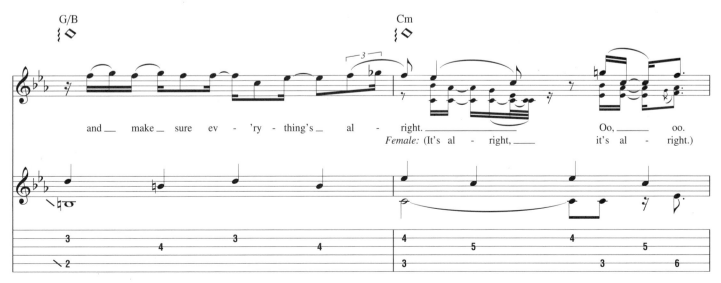

My pres-sure on your hips, ah, sink-ing my fin-ger-tips in-to

ev-'ry inch of you be-cause I know that's what you want me to do.

Outro-Chorus
Gtr. 6: w/ Rhy. Fig. 3 (till fade)
Gtr. 7: w/ Riff C
Gtr. 9 tacet

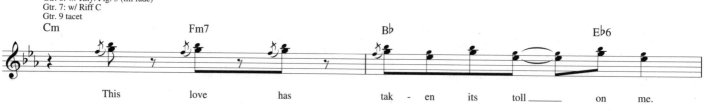

This love has tak-en its toll on me.

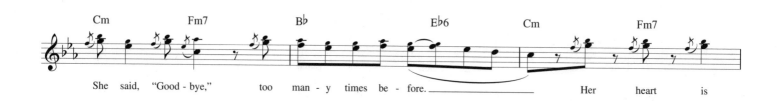

She said, "Good - bye," too man-y times be-fore. Her heart is

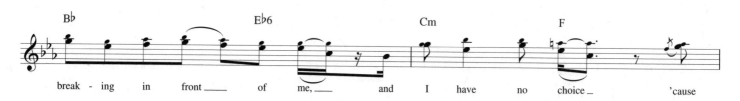

break-ing in front of me, and I have no choice 'cause

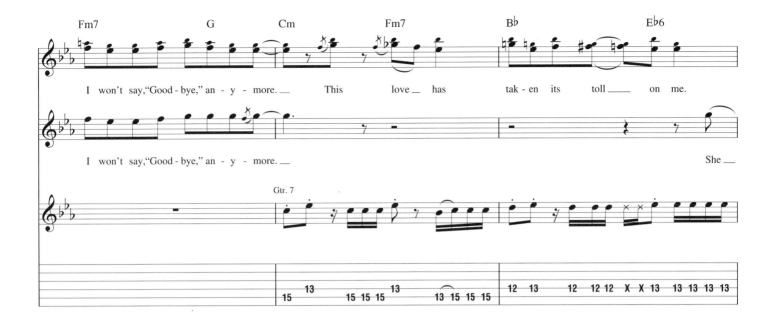

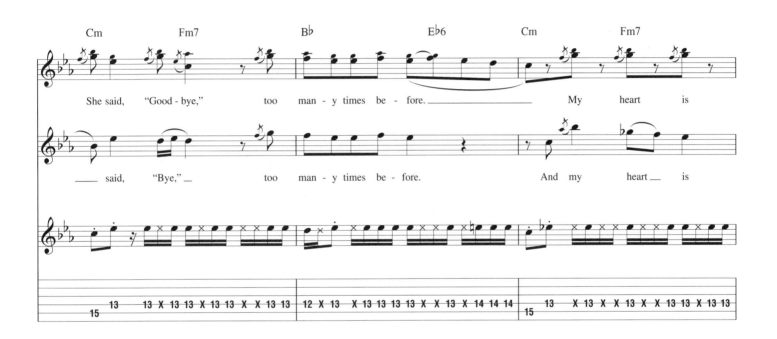

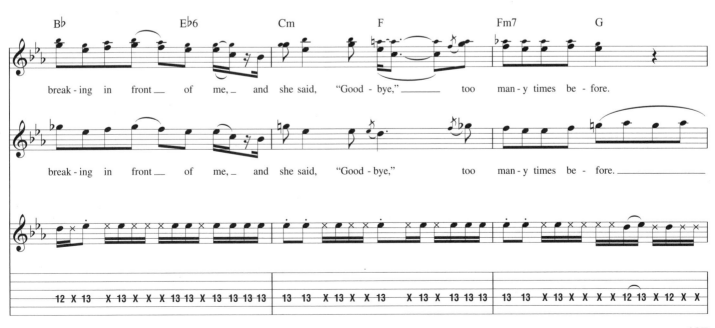

197

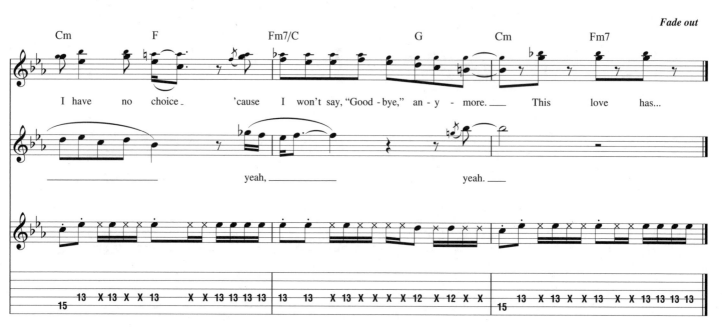

Wherever You Will Go

Words and Music by Aaron Kamin and Alex Band

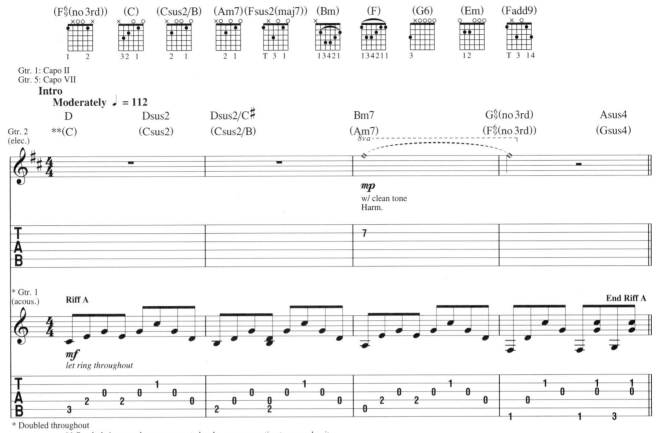

Gtr. 1: Capo II
Gtr. 5: Capo VII

Intro

Moderately ♩ = 112

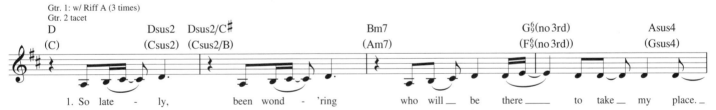

* Doubled throughout
** Symbols in parentheses represent chord names respective to capoed guitar.
Symbols above reflect actual sounding chord. Capoed fret is "0" in tab.

Verse

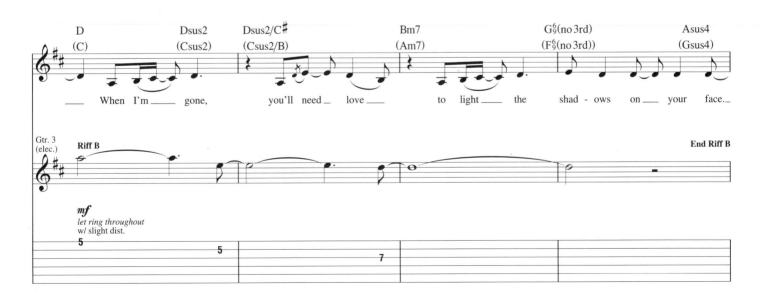

1. So late - ly, been wond - 'ring who will __ be there __ to take __ my place. __

When I'm __ gone, you'll need __ love __ to light __ the shad - ows on __ your face. __

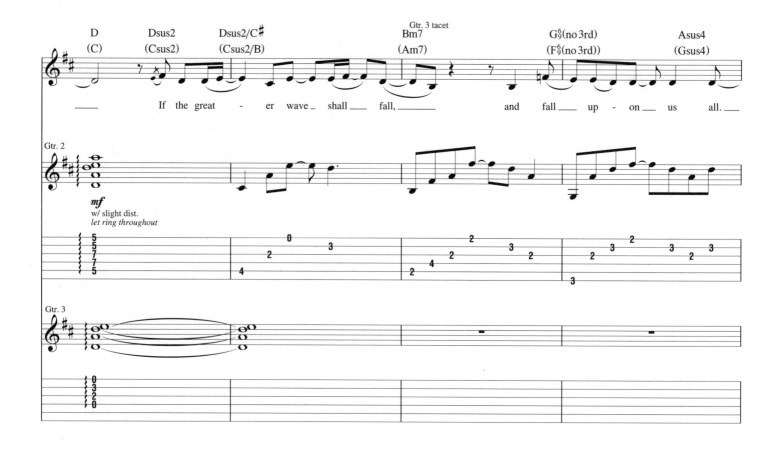

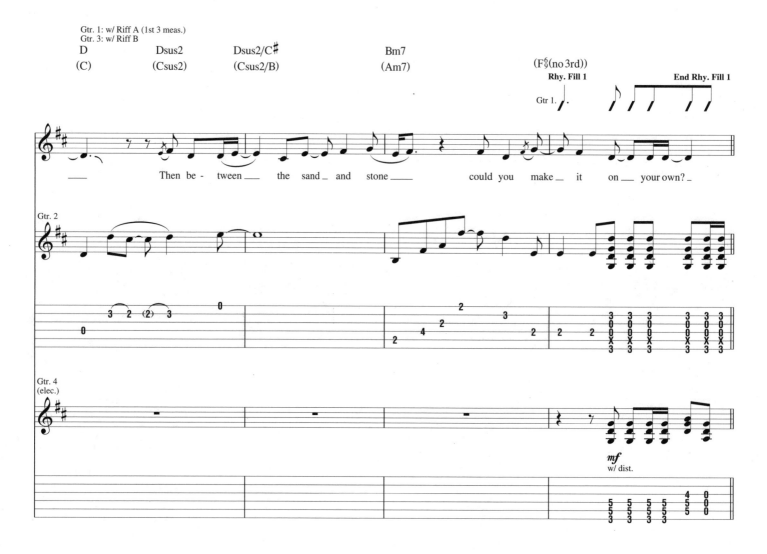

Verse

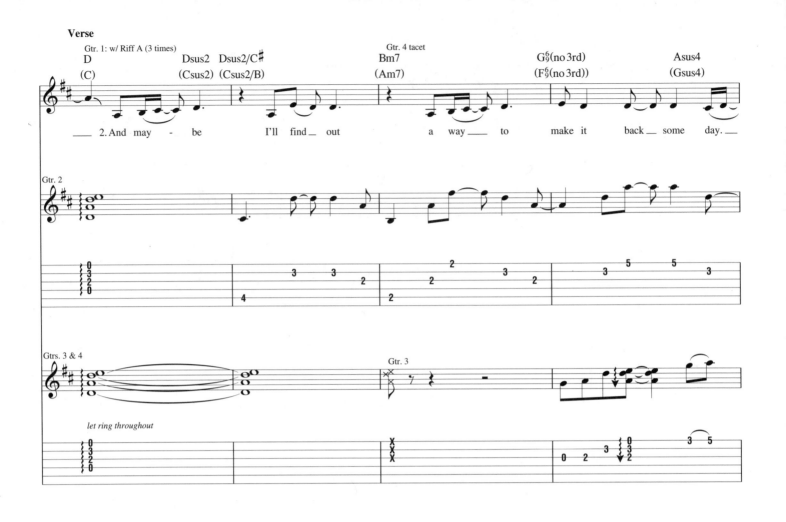

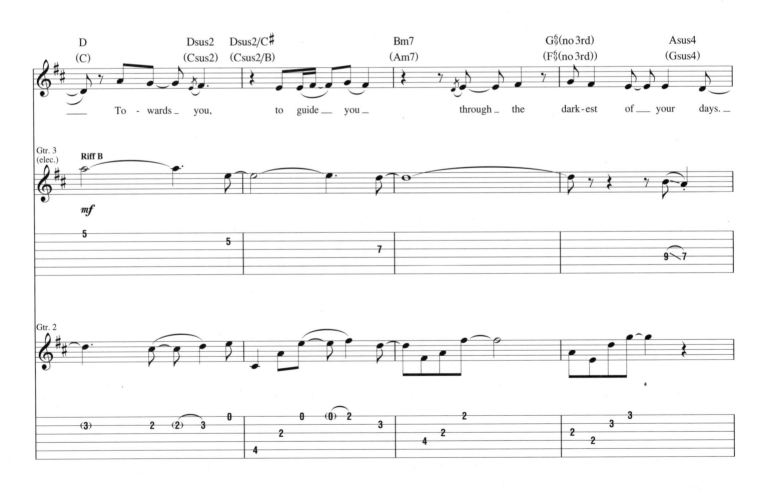

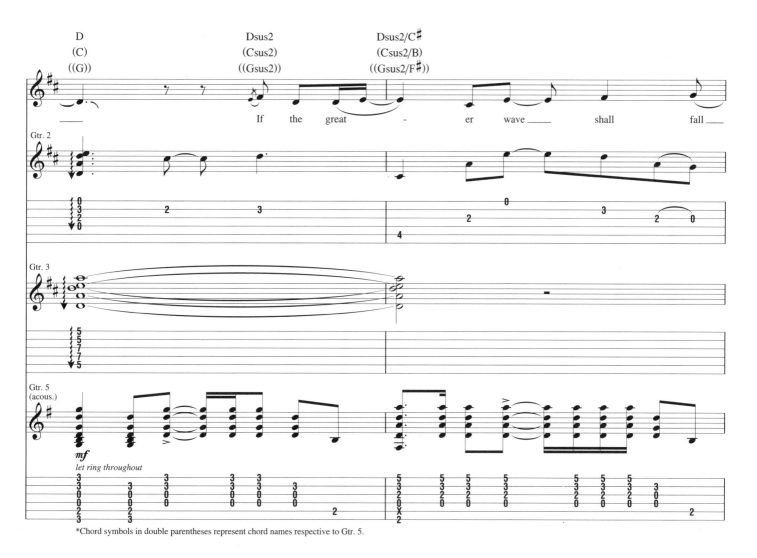

*Chord symbols in double parentheses represent chord names respective to Gtr. 5.

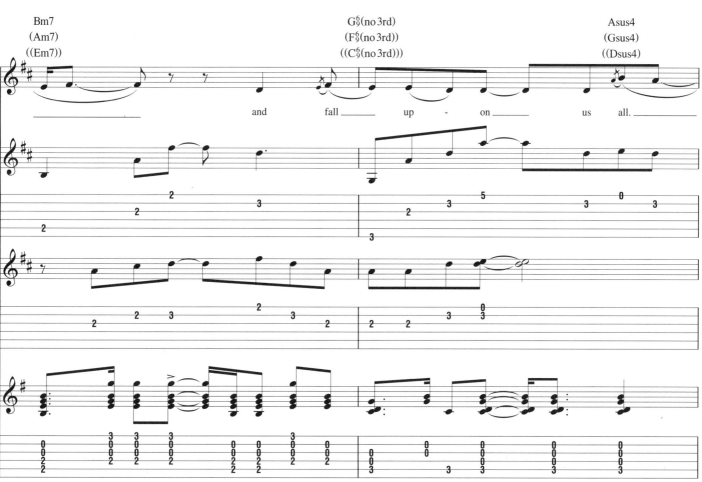

Verse

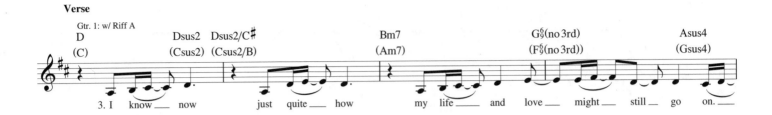

Gtr. 1: w/ Riff A

D	Dsus2 Dsus2/C#	Bm7	G6/9(no 3rd)	Asus4
(C)	(Csus2) (Csus2/B)	(Am7)	(F6/9(no 3rd))	(Gsus4)

3. I know ___ now just quite ___ how my life ___ and love ___ might ___ still ___ go ___ on. ___

Gtr. 1: w/ Riff A (1st 3 meas.)
Gtr. 3: w/ Riff B
Gtr. 5: w/ Rhy. Fig. 2

D	Dsus2	Dsus2/C#	Bm7	G6/9(no 3rd)
(C)	(Csus2)	(Csus2/B)	(Am7)	(F6/9(no 3rd))
((G))	((Gsus2))	((Gsus2/F#))	((Em7))	((C6/9(no 3rd)))

Gtr. 1: w/ Rhy. Fill 1

___ In your ___ heart, ___ in your ___ mind, ___ I'll stay ___ with you ___ for all ___ of ___ time. ___

Gtr. 2

Gtr. 4

Chorus

Gtrs. 1 & 3: w/ Rhy. Figs. 1 & 1A (5 3/4 times)
Gtrs. 2 & 4: w/ Rhy. Figs. 3 & 1B (2 7/8 times)

D	Dsus2/B	Bm7	Gsus2(maj7)
(C)	(Csus2/B)	(Am7)	(Fsus2(maj7))

___ If I ___ could, then I ___ would, I'll go ___ wher - ev - er ___ you ___ will go. ___

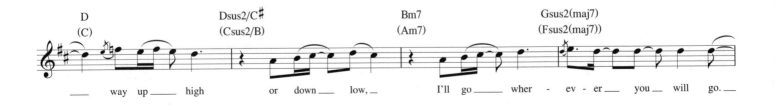

D	Dsus2/C#	Bm7	Gsus2(maj7)
(C)	(Csus2/B)	(Am7)	(Fsus2(maj7))

___ way up ___ high or down ___ low, ___ I'll go ___ wher - ev - er ___ you ___ will go. ___

Yellow

Words and Music by Guy Berryman, Jon Buckland, Will Champion and Chris Martin

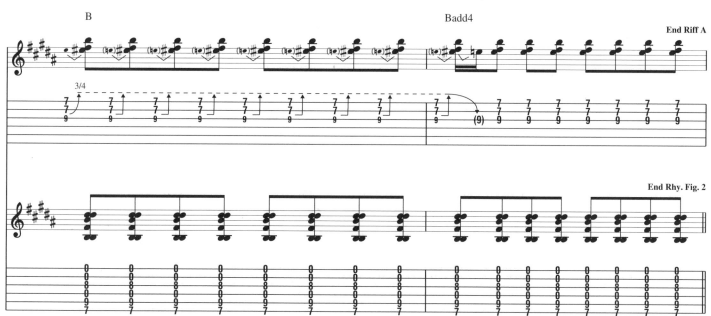

𝄋 Chorus

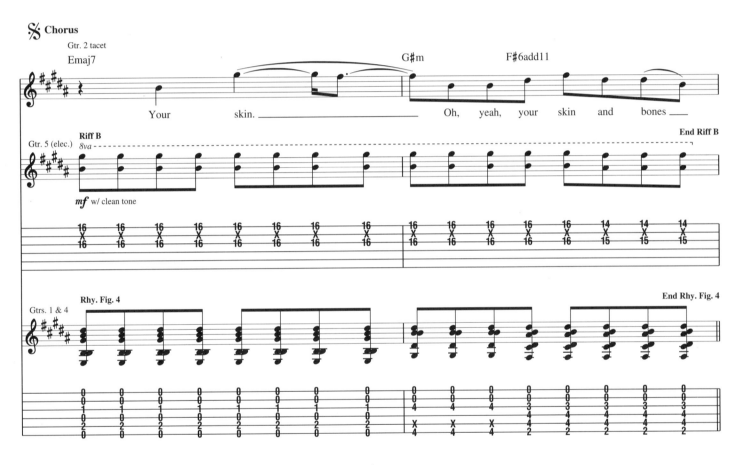

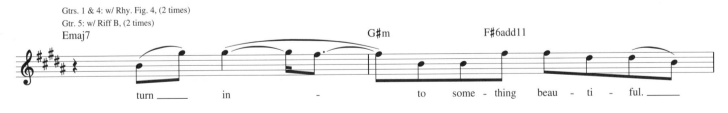

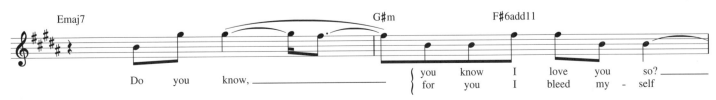

Guitar Notation Legend

Guitar Music can be notated three different ways: on a *musical staff*, in *tablature*, and in *rhythm slashes*.

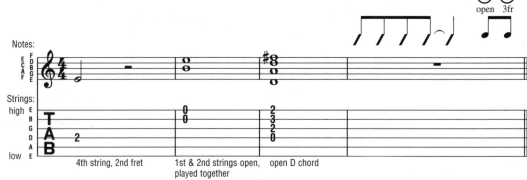

RHYTHM SLASHES are written above the staff. Strum chords in the rhythm indicated. Use the chord diagrams found at the top of the first page of the transcription for the appropriate chord voicings. Round noteheads indicate single notes.

THE MUSICAL STAFF shows pitches and rhythms and is divided by bar lines into measures. Pitches are named after the first seven letters of the alphabet.

TABLATURE graphically represents the guitar fingerboard. Each horizontal line represents a string, and each number represents a fret.

HALF-STEP BEND: Strike the note and bend up 1/2 step.

WHOLE-STEP BEND: Strike the note and bend up one step.

GRACE NOTE BEND: Strike the note and immediately bend up as indicated.

SLIGHT (MICROTONE) BEND: Strike the note and bend up 1/4 step.

BEND AND RELEASE: Strike the note and bend up as indicated, then release back to the original note. Only the first note is struck.

PRE-BEND: Bend the note as indicated, then strike it.

VIBRATO: The string is vibrated by rapidly bending and releasing the note with the fretting hand.

WIDE VIBRATO: The pitch is varied to a greater degree by vibrating with the fretting hand.

HAMMER-ON: Strike the first (lower) note with one finger, then sound the higher note (on the same string) with another finger by fretting it without picking.

PULL-OFF: Place both fingers on the notes to be sounded. Strike the first note and without picking, pull the finger off to sound the second (lower) note.

LEGATO SLIDE: Strike the first note and then slide the same fret-hand finger up or down to the second note. The second note is not struck.

SHIFT SLIDE: Same as legato slide, except the second note is struck.

TRILL: Very rapidly alternate between the notes indicated by continuously hammering on and pulling off.

TAPPING: Hammer ("tap") the fret indicated with the pick-hand index or middle finger and pull off to the note fretted by the fret hand.

NATURAL HARMONIC: Strike the note while the fret-hand lightly touches the string directly over the fret indicated.

PINCH HARMONIC: The note is fretted normally and a harmonic is produced by adding the edge of the thumb or the tip of the index finger of the pick hand to the normal pick attack.

PICK SCRAPE: The edge of the pick is rubbed down (or up) the string, producing a scratchy sound.

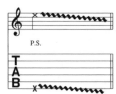

MUFFLED STRINGS: A percussive sound is produced by laying the fret hand across the string(s) without depressing, and striking them with the pick hand.

PALM MUTING: The note is partially muted by the pick hand lightly touching the string(s) just before the bridge.

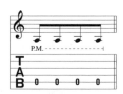

RAKE: Drag the pick across the strings indicated with a single motion.

TREMOLO PICKING: The note is picked as rapidly and continuously as possible.

VIBRATO BAR DIVE AND RETURN: The pitch of the note or chord is dropped a specified number of steps (in rhythm) then returned to the original pitch.

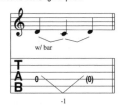

VIBRATO BAR SCOOP: Depress the bar just before striking the note, then quickly release the bar.

VIBRATO BAR DIP: Strike the note and then immediately drop a specified number of steps, then release back to the original pitch.

RECORDED VERSIONS
The Best Note-For-Note Transcriptions Available

RECORDED VERSIONS GUITAR

ALL BOOKS INCLUDE TABLATURE

00690501	Adams, Bryan – Greatest Hits	$19.95
00692015	Aerosmith – Greatest Hits	$22.95
00690178	Alice in Chains – Acoustic	$19.95
00690387	Alice in Chains – Nothing Safe: The Best of the Box	$19.95
00694932	Allman Brothers Band – Volume 1	$24.95
00694933	Allman Brothers Band – Volume 2	$24.95
00694878	Atkins, Chet – Vintage Fingerstyle	$19.95
00690418	Audio Adrenaline, Best of	$17.95
00690609	Audioslave	$19.95
00690366	Bad Company – Original Anthology, Book 1	$19.95
00690503	Beach Boys – Very Best of	$19.95
00690489	Beatles – 1	$24.95
00694929	Beatles – 1962-1966	$24.95
00694930	Beatles – 1967-1970	$24.95
00694832	Beatles – For Acoustic Guitar	$19.95
00690137	Beatles – A Hard Day's Night	$16.95
00690482	Beatles – Let It Be	$16.95
00690632	Beck – Sea Change	$19.95
00694884	Benson, George – Best of	$19.95
00692385	Berry, Chuck	$19.95
00692200	Black Sabbath – We Sold Our Soul for Rock 'N' Roll	$19.95
00690674	Blink-182	$19.95
00690389	Blink-182 – Enema of the State	$19.95
00690523	Blink-182 – Take Off Your Pants & Jacket	$19.95
00690028	Blue Oyster Cult – Cult Classics	$19.95
00690583	Boxcar Racer	$19.95
00690491	Bowie, David – Best of	$19.95
00690451	Buckley, Jeff – Collection	$24.95
00690364	Cake – Songbook	$19.95
00690564	Calling, The – Camino Palmero	$29.95
00690043	Cheap Trick – Best of	$19.95
00690567	Christian, Charlie – Definitive Collection	$19.95
00690590	Clapton, Eric – Anthology	$29.95
00692391	Clapton, Eric – Best of, 2nd Edition	$22.95
00690415	Clapton Chronicles – Best of Eric Clapton	$18.95
00690074	Clapton, Eric – The Cream of Clapton	$24.95
00694869	Clapton, Eric – Unplugged	$22.95
00690162	Clash, Best of The	$19.95
00690494	Coldplay – Parachutes	$19.95
00690593	Coldplay – A Rush of Blood to the Head	$19.95
00694940	Counting Crows – August & Everything After	$19.95
00690401	Creed – Human Clay	$19.95
00690352	Creed – My Own Prison	$19.95
00690551	Creed – Weathered	$19.95
00699521	Cure, The – Greatest Hits	$24.95
00690484	dc Talk – Intermission: The Greatest Hits	$19.95
00690289	Deep Purple, Best of	$17.95
00690563	Default – The Fallout	$19.95
00690384	Di Franco, Ani – Best of	$19.95
00695382	Dire Straits – Sultans of Swing	$19.95
00690347	Doors, The – Anthology	$22.95
00690348	Doors, The – Essential Guitar Collection	$16.95
00690555	Etheridge, Melissa – Best of	$19.95
00690524	Etheridge, Melissa – Skin	$19.95
00690515	Extreme II – Pornograffitti	$19.95
00690235	Foo Fighters – The Colour and the Shape	$19.95
00690595	Foo Fighters – One by One	$19.95
00690394	Foo Fighters – There Is Nothing Left to Lose	$19.95
00690222	G3 Live – Satriani, Vai, Johnson	$22.95
00690338	Goo Goo Dolls – Dizzy Up the Girl	$19.95
00690576	Goo Goo Dolls – Gutterflower	$19.95

00690601	Good Charlotte – The Young and the Hopeless	$19.95
00690591	Griffin, Patty – Guitar Collection	$19.95
00694798	Harrison, George – Anthology	$19.95
00692930	Hendrix, Jimi – Are You Experienced?	$24.95
00692931	Hendrix, Jimi – Axis: Bold As Love	$22.95
00690017	Hendrix, Jimi – Live at Woodstock	$24.95
00690602	Hendrix, Jimi – Smash Hits	$19.95
00660029	Holly, Buddy	$19.95
00690457	Incubus – Make Yourself	$19.95
00690544	Incubus – Morningview	$19.95
00690136	Indigo Girls – 1200 Curfews	$22.95
00694912	Johnson, Eric – Ah Via Musicom	$19.95
00690660	Johnson, Eric – Best of	$19.95
00690271	Johnson, Robert – New Transcriptions	$24.95
00699131	Joplin, Janis – Best of	$19.95
00690427	Judas Priest – Best of	$19.95
00690504	King, Albert – The Very Best of	$19.95
00690444	King, B.B. and Eric Clapton – Riding with the King	$19.95
00690339	Kinks, The – Best of	$19.95
00690614	Lavigne, Avril – Let Go	$19.95
00690525	Lynch, George – Best of	$19.95
00694755	Malmsteen, Yngwie – Rising Force	$19.95
00694956	Marley, Bob – Legend	$19.95
00690548	Marley, Bob – One Love: Very Best of	$19.95
00694945	Marley, Bob – Songs of Freedom	$24.95
00690616	Matchbox 20 – More Than You Think You Are	$19.95
00690239	Matchbox 20 – Yourself or Someone Like You	$19.95
00690382	McLachlan, Sarah – Mirrorball	$19.95
00694952	Megadeth – Countdown to Extinction	$19.95
00694951	Megadeth – Rust in Peace	$22.95
00690495	Megadeth – The World Needs a Hero	$19.95
00690505	Mellencamp, John – Guitar Collection	$19.95
00690562	Metheny, Pat – Bright Size Life	$19.95
00690559	Metheny, Pat – Question and Answer	$19.95
00690611	Nirvana	$22.95
00690189	Nirvana – From the Muddy Banks of the Wishkah	$19.95
00694913	Nirvana – In Utero	$19.95
00694883	Nirvana – Nevermind	$19.95
00690026	Nirvana – Unplugged in New York	$19.95
00690121	Oasis – (What's the Story) Morning Glory	$19.95
00690358	Offspring, The – Americana	$19.95
00690485	Offspring, The – Conspiracy of One	$19.95
00690552	Offspring, The – Ignition	$19.95
00690663	Offspring, The – Splinter	$19.95
00694847	Osbourne, Ozzy – Best of	$22.95
00690547	Osbourne, Ozzy – Down to Earth	$19.95
00690399	Osbourne, Ozzy – Ozzman Cometh	$19.95
00694855	Pearl Jam – Ten	$19.95
00690439	Perfect Circle, A – Mer De Noms	$19.95
00690499	Petty, Tom – The Definitive Guitar Collection	$19.95
00690424	Phish – Farmhouse	$19.95
00690240	Phish – Hoist	$19.95
00690607	Phish – Round Room	$19.95
00690331	Phish – Story of the Ghost	$19.95
00690642	Pillar – Fireproof	$19.95
00690428	Pink Floyd – Dark Side of the Moon	$19.95
00690546	P.O.D. – Satellite	$19.95
00693864	Police, The – Best of	$19.95
00690299	Presley, Elvis – Best of Elvis: The King of Rock 'n' Roll	$19.95
00694975	Queen – Greatest Hits	$24.95
00694910	Rage Against the Machine	$19.95

00690145	Rage Against the Machine – Evil Empire	$19.95
00690426	Ratt – Best of	$19.95
00690055	Red Hot Chili Peppers – Bloodsugarsexmagik	$19.95
00690584	Red Hot Chili Peppers – By the Way	$19.95
00690379	Red Hot Chili Peppers – Californication	$19.95
00690090	Red Hot Chili Peppers – One Hot Minute	$22.95
00690511	Reinhardt, Django – Definitive Collection	$19.95
00690643	Relient K – Two Lefts Don't Make a Right...But Three Do	$19.95
00690014	Rolling Stones – Exile on Main Street	$24.95
00690631	Rolling Stones – Guitar Anthology	$24.95
00690600	Saliva – Back Into Your System	$19.95
00690031	Santana's Greatest Hits	$19.95
00690566	Scorpions – Best of	$19.95
00690604	Seger, Bob – Guitar Collection	$19.95
00690419	Slipknot	$19.95
00690530	Slipknot – Iowa	$19.95
00690385	Sonicflood	$19.95
00690021	Sting – Fields of Gold	$19.95
00690597	Stone Sour	$19.95
00690520	Styx Guitar Collection	$19.95
00690519	Sum 41 – All Killer No Filler	$19.95
00690612	Sum 41 – Does This Look Infected?	$19.95
00690425	System of a Down	$19.95
00690606	System of a Down – Steal This Album	$19.95
00690531	System of a Down – Toxicity	$19.95
00694824	Taylor, James – Best of	$16.95
00690238	Third Eye Blind	$19.95
00690580	311 – From Chaos	$19.95
00690295	Tool – Aenima	$19.95
00690654	Train – Best of	$19.95
00690039	Vai, Steve – Alien Love Secrets	$24.95
00690392	Vai, Steve – The Ultra Zone	$19.95
00690370	Vaughan, Stevie Ray and Double Trouble – The Real Deal: Greatest Hits Volume 2	$22.95
00690116	Vaughan, Stevie Ray – Guitar Collection	$24.95
00660058	Vaughan, Stevie Ray – Lightnin' Blues 1983-1987	$24.95
00690550	Vaughan, Stevie Ray and Double Trouble – Live at Montreux 1982 & 1985	$24.95
00694835	Vaughan, Stevie Ray – The Sky Is Crying	$22.95
00690015	Vaughan, Stevie Ray – Texas Flood	$19.95
00694789	Waters, Muddy – Deep Blues	$24.95
00690071	Weezer (The Blue Album)	$19.95
00690516	Weezer (The Green Album)	$19.95
00690579	Weezer – Maladroit	$19.95
00690286	Weezer – Pinkerton	$19.95
00690447	Who, The – Best of	$24.95
00690640	Wilcox, David – Anthology 2000-2003	$19.95
00690320	Williams, Dar – Best of	$17.95
00690596	Yardbirds, The – Best of	$19.95
00690443	Zappa, Frank – Hot Rats	$19.95
00690589	ZZ Top Guitar Anthology	$22.95

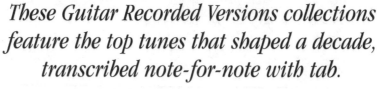

THE DECADE SERIES

*These Guitar Recorded Versions collections
feature the top tunes that shaped a decade,
transcribed note-for-note with tab.*

The 1950s

35 pivotal songs from the early rock years: All Shook Up • Donna • Heartbreak Hotel • Hound Dog • I'm Movin' On • Lonesome Town • Matchbox • Moonlight in Vermont • My Babe • Poor Little Fool • Race With the Devil • Rebel 'Rouser • Rock Around the Clock • Rockin' Robin • Sleepwalk • Slippin' and Slidin' • Sweet Little Angel • Tequila • Wake Up Little Susie • Yankee Doodle Dixie • and more.

00690543..$14.95

The 1960s

30 songs that defined the '60s: Badge • Blackbird • Fun, Fun, Fun • Gloria • Good Lovin' • Happy Together • Hey Joe • Hush • I Can See for Miles • I Feel Fine • I Get Around • Louie, Louie • My Girl • Oh, Pretty Woman • On the Road Again • Somebody to Love • Soul Man • Suite: Judy Blue Eyes • Susie-Q • Wild Thing • and more.

00690542..$14.95

The 1970s

30 top songs from the '70s: Best of My Love • Breakdown • Dust in the Wind • Evil Woman • Landslide • Lay Down Sally • Let It Be • Maggie May • No Woman No Cry • Oye Como Va • Show Me the Way • Smoke on the Water • So Into You • Space Oddity • Stayin' Alive • Teach Your Children • Time in a Bottle • Walk This Way • Wheel in the Sky • You've Got a Friend • and more.

00690541..$15.95

The 1980s

30 songs that best represent the decade: 867-5309/Jenny • Every Breath You Take • Eye of the Tiger • Fight for Your Right (To Party) • Heart and Soul • Hit Me With Your Best Shot • I Love Rock 'N Roll • La Bamba • Money for Nothing • Mony, Mony • Refugee • Rock Me • Rock You Like a Hurricane • Start Me Up • Summer of '69 • Sweet Child O' Mine • Wait • What I Like About You • and more.

00690540..$15.95

The 1990s

30 essential '90s classics: All I Wanna Do • Barely Breathing • Building a Mystery • Come Out and Play • Cryin' • Fields of Gold • Friends in Low Places • Hold My Hand • I Can't Dance • Iris • Jump, Jive an' Wail • More Than Words • Santa Monica • Semi-Charmed Life • Silent Lucidity • Smells Like Teen Spirit • Smooth • Tears in Heaven • Two Princes • Under the Bridge • Wonderwall • and more.

00690539..$15.95

The 2000s

30 songs, including: Alive • All the Small Things • Are You Gonna Be My Girl • Californication • Click Click Boom • Complicated • Drive • Hanging by a Moment • Heaven • If You're Gone • Kryptonite • Lifestyles of the Rich and Famous • Maps • The Space Between • Take a Look Around (Theme from *M:I-2*) • Wherever You Will Go • Yellow • and more.

00690761..$14.95

More of the 1950s

30 top songs of the '50s, including: Blue Suede Shoes • Bye Bye Love • Don't Be Cruel (To a Heart That's True) • Hard Headed Woman • Jailhouse Rock • La Bamba • Peggy Sue • Rawhide • Say Man • See You Later, Alligator • That'll Be the Day • Yakety Yak • and more.

00690756..$14.95

More of the 1960s

30 great songs of the '60s: All Along the Watchtower • Born to Be Wild • Brown Eyed Girl • California Dreamin' • Do You Believe in Magic • Hang On Sloopy • I'm a Believer • Paperback Writer • Secret Agent Man • So You Want to Be a Rock and Roll Star • Sunshine of Your Love • Surfin' U.S.A. • Ticket to Ride • Travelin' Man • White Rabbit • With a Little Help from My Friends • and more.

00690757..$14.95

More of the 1970s

30 more hits from the '70s: Aqualung • Carry on Wayward Son • Evil Ways • Feel like Makin' Love • Fly like an Eagle • Give a Little Bit • I Want You to Want Me • Lights • My Sharona • One Way or Another • Rock and Roll All Nite • Roxanne • Saturday Night's Alright (For Fighting) • Suffragette City • Sultans of Swing • Sweet Emotion • Sweet Home Alabama • Won't Get Fooled Again • Wonderful Tonight • and more.

00690758..$14.95

More of the 1980s

30 songs that defined the decade: Call Me • Crazy Crazy Nights • Heartbreaker • Here I Go Again • It's Still Rock and Roll to Me • Jack and Diane • Jessie's Girl • Once Bitten Twice Shy • Rock the Casbah • Runnin' Down a Dream • Sharp Dressed Man • Smokin' in the Boys Room • Stray Cat Strut • Wanted Dead or Alive • White Wedding • and more.

00690759..$14.95

More of the 1990s

30 songs: Alive • Change the World • Come as You Are • The Freshmen • Hard to Handle • Hole Hearted • Just a Girl • Lightning Crashes • Mr. Jones • No Excuses • No Rain • Only Wanna Be with You • Pretty Fly (For a White Guy) • Push • Shimmer • Stay • Stupid Girl • What I Got • Whatever • Whiskey in the Jar • Zombie • and more.

00690760..$14.95

More of the 2000s

30 recent hits: All Downhill From Here • By the Way • Clocks • Cold Hard Bitch • Drops of Jupiter (Tell Me) • Harder to Breathe • I Did It • I Hate Everything About You • Learn to Fly • Ocean Avenue • St. Anger • Wasting My Time • When I'm Gone • Wish You Were Here • With Arms Wide Open • Youth of the Nation • and more.

00690762..$14.95

FOR MORE INFORMATION, SEE YOUR LOCAL MUSIC DEALER,
OR WRITE TO:

HAL•LEONARD®
CORPORATION

7777 W. BLUEMOUND RD. P.O. BOX 13819 MILWAUKEE, WI 53213

www.halleonard.com

Prices, contents and availability subject to change without notice.

11/04